John & Sally McKennas' Guides
The 100 Best Places to Stay in Ireland

2013 EDITION

*www.guides.ie*

McKENNAS' GUIDES

# 100 BEST
## PLACES TO STAY
## IN IRELAND 2013

**JOHN MCKENNA - SALLY MCKENNA**

Withdrawn from Stock

ESTRAGON PRESS

FIRST PUBLISHED IN FEBRUARY 2013
BY ESTRAGON PRESS
DURRUS
COUNTY CORK
© ESTRAGON PRESS

TEXT © JOHN & SALLY MCKENNA
THE MORAL RIGHT OF THE AUTHORS HAS BEEN ASSERTED

978-1-906927-13-4


ILLUSTRATIONS BY AOIFE WASSER

PRINTED IN SPAIN BY GRAPHYCEMS

**WRITTEN & EDITED** BY JOHN MCKENNA

**CONTRIBUTING EDITORS:**

EAMON BARRETT

WILLIAM BARRY

CAROLINE BYRNE

AOIFE COX

ELIZABETH FIELD

CAROLINE HENNESSY

CONNIE MCKENNA

LESLIE WILLIAMS

**PUBLISHING EDITOR:** SALLY MCKENNA

**EDITOR:** JUDITH CASEY

**EDITORIAL ASSISTANT
& WEB PICTURE EDITOR:** EVE CLANCY

**WEB:** FLUIDEDGE.IE

FOR:

Edwina Murray

WITH SPECIAL THANKS TO

John Masterson, Grainne Byrne, Julie Barrett,
George Lane, Frank McKevitt, Hugh Stancliffe,
Dr Denis Cotter, Sam McKenna, PJ McKenna.
And to the wonderful team at Gill & Macmillan.

The McKennas' Guides have been published in Ireland for almost twenty-five years. During this time our productions have expanded to include digitial guides, a website and, more recently, a video channel.

## We are in print

*The Irish Food Guide* - the tenth edition extends to 700 pages of the finest food to be found throughout Ireland.

*The 100 Best Restaurants in Ireland 2013* - the companion edition to this volume featuring the most creative, dynamic and original restaurateurs throughout Ireland.

We also publish cookery books, see our website www.guides.ie for titles and to order.

## We are on Social Media

Facebook: https://www.facebook.com/BridgestoneGuides
Twitter: @McKennasGuides

## We are on the web

Find us at *www.guides.ie*, where you can keep up-to-date with what is happening in Irish food and also access our publications on line.

## We publish a Who's Who

The key personalities in modern Irish food are profiled in our *Who's Who of Irish Food*.

## We send out a regular newsletter

Sign up for our *Megabites* Newsletter for up-to-date reviews, features and slide shows.

## We make short films about food

Our short video films profile key people and events in Ireland's contemporary food culture: www.youtube.com/user/irishfoodchannel

So, we are chairing a conference on food and tourism up in County Mayo, and there are two stats that make our jaws drop, and our eyes water.

• The regular amateur European athlete who takes part in triathlons earns, on average €160,000 per annum.

• Thanks to its pioneering work in establishing the Great Western Greenway, the Mulranny Park added 1,000 bednights to its annual turnover.

• And everyone in the audience thought , "Send me your tired triathletes, send me your Greenway walkers..."

• In the companion guide to this book, the *100 Best Restaurants 2013*, we have argued that today a chef has to be holistic: if all he or she does is cook, then they are doomed.

• For people in hospitality, the need to have an holistic offer is even more urgent. You need loop walks, and surf schools. You need equestrianism and kayak foraging. You need cycle tracks and hiking guides. You need culture trails and you need places where surfers can dry their wetsuits. It's not enough to know the weather: you also need to know the waves, the wind, the stars and who makes the best martini in the local pubs.

• Holistic hospitality is what is today needed to succeed, in order to have the €160k guy driving down your road with his €5k bike on the back of the car. There are no accidental tourists anymore: everybody wants everything.

John McKenna, Durrus, West Cork, February 2013

> "Jump out of yourself. Don't do what others do. Grow the business organically: quick fixes don't last. Take on a new project each year".
>
> Paul Carroll, Ghan House,
> Carlingford, County Louth

• One of the main speakers at the Westport conference we referred to in our Introduction was Paul Carroll, of Ghan House. Mr Carroll is one of the smartest thinkers in modern hospitality, and we quote some of his aphorisms – hastily scribbled in our notebook as he spoke – to show the sort of clever thinking that has helped him deliver such success to Ghan House – Ghan is operating at a higher rate of occupancy and dining today than it was enjoying back in 2007, at the height of the boom.

• For us, one of the key points Mr Carroll made is the idea that one should have a new project every year to drive the business forward. This is something that all the best practitioners subscribe to, quietly, patiently, so that if you return to Ghan House, or to Kelly's Resort Hotel, or to Ballymaloe House, there will have been an improvement since your last trip, some development, some tweaking, a project begun and completed and up-and-running. Hospitality thrives on the challenge of the new, and all the best guys know that.

# hot

# classic

# new

Something new

• *The 100 Best Places to Stay in Ireland* is arranged alphabetically, by county, so it begins with County Carlow, which is followed by County Cavan, and so on. Within the counties, the entries are once again listed alphabetically. Entries in Northern Ireland are itemised alphabetically, at the end of the book. All NI prices are quoted in sterling.

• The contents of the *100 Best Guides* are exclusively the result of the authors' deliberations. All meals and accommodation were paid for and any offers of discounts or gifts were refused.

• Many of the places featured in this book are only open during the summer, which means that they can be closed for any given length of time between October and March.

• **PRICES:** Average prices are calculated on the basis of one night's stay for bed and breakfast. Prices are subject to change, and therefore can only represent a guideline.

• **LISTINGS:** In every entry in the book we try to list address, telephone number, and internet details. We also request details of disabled access, plus any other relevant information.

• **GPS CO-ORDINATES:** We have printed co-ordinates as provided to us by the various establishments. The *McKennas' Guides*, however, can accept no responsibility for the ultimate accuracy of the co-ordinates provided to us.

• **TELEPHONE NUMBERS:** Telephone numbers are listed using the international dialling code. If you are calling a number within the country, omit the international code and use the 0.

• **McKENNAS' GUIDES PLAQUES:** Look out for the current year of our McKennas' Plaques, displayed by many of our listed establishments.

# KILGRANEY COUNTRY HOUSE

**Bryan Leech & Martin Marley**
**Bagenalstown**
**County Carlow**
📞 +353 (0) 59-977 5283
✉ info@kilgraneyhouse.com
🖰 www.kilgraneyhouse.com

## Stylish and enigmatic, Kilgraney is one of the most distinctive of the Irish country houses.

'It is a thoroughly modern country house hotel', wrote the great food writer Annie Bell, way back in 1999 when she first visited Bryan and Martin's Kilgraney House, not long after the guys opened their doors. 'The cooking,' said Ms Bell, 'sings with wonderfully clear notes'. Claire Goodwillie of the McKennas' Guides agrees: her most recent meal at Kilgraney won a single word of praise: 'wonderful'. Nowhere else is quite like Kilgraney, nowhere else has such a finely tuned aesthetic in every aspect of the operation, nowhere else has such ageless modernity, such a powerful sense of feng shui gracing every element of the operation. You have to applaud the fact that the house itself has changed little over the years, because Martin and Bryan got it so right at the start that it hasn't needed to be tampered with. Vitally, Bryan Leech's cooking remains amongst the most intuitive and yet polished country house cooking you can enjoy anywhere. When you marry that smart cooking with the sense of style that blesses Kilgraney House, then you have a true Irish classic, a world-class Irish country destination.

- **OPEN:** Mar-Nov, Wed-Sun
- **ROOMS:** Six double rooms & two courtyard suites
- **PRICE:** B&B €85-€120 per person sharing.

- **NOTES:** Visa, Mastercard, Amex, Laser. Dinner, 8pm, €50 (Six course), book by noon. ♿Disabled access with assistance, please phone to discuss needs. Aroma Spa. Mid-week and aromatherapy packages available. Children over 12 only.

- **DIRECTIONS:**
Just off the R705, 6km from Bagenalstown.
GPS 52.653333 -6.957222

# STEP HOUSE HOTEL

James & Cait Coady
Main Street, Borris
County Carlow
☏ +353 59 977 1624
✉ info@stephousehotel.ie
🖱 www.stephousehotel.ie

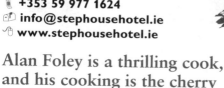

Alan Foley is a thrilling cook,
and his cooking is the cherry
on the lovely Step House cake.

Some chefs have such a precise technique at their disposal
that it serves to define their cooking. The technique be-
gets the textures and tastes, and serves as the foundation
of their food. Graham Neville has it. Paul Flynn has it. And
Alan Foley of the Step House has it.

Mr Foley cooks beautifully, and precisely. Look at the
changes he rings in tastes and textures with his lamb
tasting plate, or his warm poached lobster, or his amazing
strawberry consommé. The dishes are tactile, varied and
hugely pleasing and whilst they have all the other neces-
sities - he sources well, he presents well, the staff serve
well - it is the finesse of his culinary technique that makes
the cooking so delicious, so enjoyable, so memorable.
His poached lobster is sublime; lamb loin is cooked pink,
the shoulder slow-cooked and formed into a terrine, a
basil purée and fresh Ardsallagh goat's cheese flecked
about the plate with painterly precision. Hereford beef
offers beef fillet and braised ox cheek, with spring onion
hollandaise and it's a riot of umami-ness. Puddings are a
joy to behold and to devour. A great destination.

- **OPEN:** All year
- **ROOMS:** 20 bedrooms
- **PRICE:** B&B from €65-€85 per person sharing.
Single supplement €10

- **NOTES:** Visa, Mastercard, Laser. ♿Disabled
access. 1808 Bar lunch & dinner, 12.20pm-2pm, 6pm-
9.30pm. Rubens Restaurant opens Fri & Sat, 6pm-9pm

- **DIRECTIONS:**
Borris is in between Carlow and Kilkenny, and the
hotel is on the main street in the village.
GPS 52.601244 -6.927553

# MACNEAN TOWNHOUSE

**Neven & Amelda Maguire**
**Blacklion**
**County Cavan**

📞 +353 71 985 3022
✉ info@macneanrestaurant.com
🖰 www.macneanrestaurant.com

## The cooking in the MacNean woke every sense in Leslie Williams' being. Book a room.

'What do you do if you find yourself passing through Blacklion in Cavan, at 8pm on a Sunday evening, and you are starving hungry?' asks Leslie Williams.

Why you simply stop into MacNean Restaurant and plead hunger. 'Feed me!' you plead.

They explain very gently that the restaurant is full and you look wan, and hang your lip a little. But, it's ok because they quickly say 'But don't worry: we won't turn you away, and if you don't mind eating in the bar area we would be happy to help.'

'What follows is a range of courses of beautifully cooked food (many of which are not even mentioned on the menu) that woke every sense and made my skin bristle. This was not just food but a return to the origins of the original idea of a restaurant – a place that restores you. Not just your faith in what a good meal can do, but probably in humanity as well.'

Wow! What an experience! Hunger sated. Appetite satisfied. Faith restored. Then upstairs to bed and the good sleep in one of the MacNean's lovely, cosy, comfy rooms.

● **OPEN:** All year, except January
● **ROOMS:** 17 rooms
● **PRICE:** B&B €67-€96 per person sharing

● **NOTES:** Visa, Mastercard, Laser. MacNean Restaurant open 6pm-9.30pm Wed-Sat; 1pm & 3.30pm, 7pm-8.30pm Sun (closed Wed low season). Sun Lunch €39, Dinner €67-€82.
Recommended for vegetarians.

● **DIRECTIONS:**
On the main street in Blacklion.
GPS 54.291361 -7.877739

# THE OLDE POST INN

**Tara McCann & Gearoid Lynch**
**Cloverhill, Butler's Bridge**
**County Cavan**

📠 **+353 47 55555**
📧 **info@theoldepostinn.com**
🖰 **www.theoldepostinn.com**

The OP is at the forefront of the locavore revolution, so come and enjoy local foods cooked by Gearoid.

'Seventy five percent of what I cook comes now comes from within a 10-mile range of the restaurant,' Gearoid Lynch told a Eurotoques award ceremony. Mr Lynch's statement is one of the great chicken-and-egg stories: are the producers there because of The Olde Post, or is The Olde Post there because of the producers? We suspect it is the former: Mr Lynch has created an aureola of suppliers because he has fashioned such a brilliant restaurant with rooms, a destination overseen with assured poise by Tara McCann. Together, they have shown that building a restaurant with a great reputation also builds a thriving local economy, and they have also shown that a restaurant and an economy together build a culture.

The produce of these great local producers shines in great, confident, grown-up cooking. Mr Lynch could cook the 'phone directory for us and we would be happy, such is his culinary mastery. But, to be honest, what we want is home smoked chicken salad with tarragon, and Olde Post smokies, and wild venison with Valrhona sauce, and chocolate mocha torte. Good rooms make for the perfect getaway.

- ● **OPEN:** all year, except Christmas
- ● **ROOMS:** Six double rooms.
- ● **PRICE:** B&B €100 per double room

- ● **NOTES:** Olde Post Inn restaurant open 6pm-9pm Tue-Thu, 6pm-9.30pm Fri-Sat, 12.30pm-2.30pm, 5.30pm-8.30pm Sun. Dinner €55, Sun Lunch €33. ♿ No disabled access.

- ● **DIRECTIONS:**
From Cavan follow N3. At Butler's Bridge, take the N54 and the Olde Post is 3km further, on the right. GPS 54.0801 -7.3701

# GREGAN'S CASTLE

**Simon & Freddy Haden**
**Ballyvaughan**
**County Clare**
📱 **+353 65 707 7005**
📠 **stay@gregans.ie**
🖰 **www.gregans.ie**

Every detail in Gregan's Castle matches the tone poem aesthetic of this singular hotel.

Everything in Simon and Freddy's extraordinary Gregan's Castle seems to float with the ease and grace of a note of music moving through air. The setting; the architecture; the design; the aesthetic; David Hurley's inspired cooking; the welcome, all conjoin to make for one of the greatest experiences in Irish hospitality, and there are times here when you can feel you are in a work of art, rather than simply staying at an hotel. Freddy's design plays an enormous part in creating this effect, for here is a house – so rare in Ireland! – where every object and every object is in exactly the right place. Mr Hurley worked his way to the top job in the kitchen, which meant his food had the maturity and mellifluousness it needed right from day one, and he will surely be one the cooks of the decade. Some cooks foreground themselves in their cooking, but Mr Hurley effectively disappears into his cooking: the food takes over completely. As a key element of the aesthetic of Gregan's Castle, it is hard to imagine cooking that could be more appropriate, or more sublime. Amazingly, Gregan's seems to hit new peaks and then transcend them.

● **OPEN:** 14 Feb-16 November
● **ROOMS:** 21 rooms and suites
● **PRICE:** €170-€325 per room

● **NOTES:** Dinner served 6pm-9pm Mon- Tues, Thur-Sat. Bar Dinner 5pm-8pm Wed & Sun. Bar lunch everyday 12.30pm-2.30pm. Afternoon Tea 2.30pm-4.30pm. Burren tours arranged. ♿ Disabled access. Croquet lawn.

● **DIRECTIONS:**
3.5 miles outside Ballyvaughan village.
GPS 53.076944 -9.186222

## HOTEL DOOLIN

**Donal Minihane (General Manager)**
**Doolin**
**County Clare**
📞 + 353 65 707 4111
📧 info@hoteldoolin.ie
🖱 www.hoteldoolin.ie

A smart collaboration of functions is the USP of the fine Hotel Doolin.

*Something new*

Can a building multi-task? Can you say to an inanimate construction: okay, you are the shop. And you are the bar. And you'll be the restaurant. And you over there, – yes, you – you will be the booking office. Who's left? Oh yeah: you're the reception area for the hotel, and you'll be adjacent to the café, is that o.k.? Everybody happy. Right so, let's call ourselves – collectively – the Hotel Doolin. OK, let's go to work. Hotel Doolin does all this, and it does it smartly and economically. Rather than having lots of working compartments in the building, it frontloads the offer: there in front of you is the shop, the café, the bar, the restaurant, the reception area, the booking office. It's an hotel, but not as we know it. And, now, there is a pair of smart guys – chef Peter Jackson; manager Donal Minihane – who have gotten this smart concept by the scruff of the neck and are working hard to create a destination. Mr Jackson cooks well: his food is clean and lean and he cooks fish and shellfish confidently, and has a polytunnel in clear sight to give him interesting leaves and queer gear. Breakfast, incidentally, is a ginormous feast.

● **OPEN:** All year, except Christmas Day
● **ROOMS:** 17 rooms
● **PRICE:** €65 per person sharing, B&B

● **NOTES:**  Chervil Restaurant, Fitzpatrick's Bar, Café Sonas, Shaggy Sheep Gift Shop & Gallery, Doolin Pantry, Tourist Information Bureau.
♿ Disabled access.

● **DIRECTIONS:**
Follow the coast road from Ballyvaughan, turning right towards Doolin after approx 16km. The hotel is in the centre of the village.

# TAKE AFTERNOON TEA

### 1
**ARIEL HOUSE**
**COUNTY DUBLIN**

### 2
**THE CARRIAGE HOUSE**
**NORTHERN IRELAND**

### 3
**COOPERSHILL HOUSE**
**COUNTY SLIGO**

### 4
**THE GLEN**
**COUNTY CORK**

### 5
**GREGAN'S CASTLE**
**COUNTY CLARE**

### 6
**KNOCKEVEN**
**COUNTY CORK**

### 7
**THE HERON'S REST**
**COUNTY GALWAY**

### 8
**PEMBROKE TOWNHOUSE**
**COUNTY DUBLIN**

### 9
**NUMBER ONE PERY SQUARE**
**COUNTY LIMERICK**

### 10
**RICHMOND HOUSE**
**COUNTY WATERFORD**

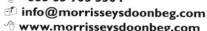

## MORRISSEY'S

**Hugh Morrissey**
**Doonbeg**
**County Clare**
🕯 **+353 65 905 5304**
📧 **info@morrisseysdoonbeg.com**
🖱 **www.morrisseysdoonbeg.com**

# The quintessential dinner'n'duvet destination in south County Clare, Morrissey's is a peach.

Hugh Morrissey has transformed this lovely pub from a traditional Irish bar into a svelte restaurant with rooms, yet he has somehow managed to keep the graceful ambience of the old place, where four generations of the Morrissey family have plied their trade.

The cooking in Morrissey's is modern and informal – chicken Caesar salad; Angus beef burger; salmon and cod fish cake; home-made scampi with tartare sauce – food that you can relax with, food that all the family can and will enjoy. That relaxed air is worth dwelling on, for it's really the signature of Morrissey's, a destination that enjoys a youthful, laid-back sang-froid that is hard to resist. We have remarked before on the incredible feat that Hugh Morrissey has performed in his stylish 'dinner'n'duvet', transforming it from a simple family-run pub that was open for only a few months of the year into a dynamic 'D'n'D' that now opens fully for ten months of the year. Morrissey's is yet another excellent restaurant with rooms, the sort of thing they do with style, creativity and panache, here in the Banner County.

- **OPEN:** March-Dec
- **ROOMS:** Seven rooms
- **PRICE:** B&B €90 per room, €50 single

- **NOTES:** Visa, Mastercard, Laser, Amex. Pub restaurant opens for lunch, 12.30pm-2.30pm, and dinner, 6pm-9.30pm, €35. (Closed Sun evening)

- **DIRECTIONS:**
From Ennis, follow the Kilrush road. In Kilrush follow signs for Kilkee, and then look for the Doonbeg sign. The pub is right beside the bridge in the centre of the village. GPS 52.730861 -9.524353

## MOUNT VERNON

**Ally Raftery & Mark Helmore**
**Flaggy Shore, New Quay,**
**Burren, County Clare**
📱 **+353 65 707 8126**
✉ **info@mountvernon.ie**
🖰 **www.mountvernon.ie**

Mount Vernon is spiffing, a great house that pulses with a vivid, creative energy.

'Mount Vernon is a house of true beauty', says Connie McKenna. One of its secrets is that it shows the importance of travel as, everywhere you look, an artefact collected from Asia, Africa, South America, or elsewhere is to be found in exactly the right place within the room. The genius, however, is that it's not cluttered – it's almost as if all the ornaments ran into the house and chose their own space, their favourite place. Paintings and concave mirrors are scattered across the walls. The living room, in particular, is a place where you can find your heart in true comfort. The food is simply delightful: fish broth with prawns, lemon and dill nourishes the soul inside out. Halibut, juicy to the bone is served with new potatoes and colourful, well-cooked vegetables. This is what simple, honest, home cooking is about. To top things beautifully, Ally's homemade apple pie was country cooking at its most delightful: every mouthful took our palates on a journey. Mount Vernon fits beautifully with the wild Flaggy Shore – Ally and Mark have made a special place here, so make sure to stay a few nights and get it in your soul.

● **OPEN:** 1 April-31 Oct, or by arrangement
● **ROOMS:** Five rooms, all en suite or with private bathroom
● **PRICE:** B&B €90-€115 per person sharing. €30 single supplement

● **NOTES:** Visa, Mastercard, Laser. Guided walks and fishing can be arranged. ♿ No disabled access.

● **DIRECTIONS:**
Signposted at two points from the main Ballyvaughan-Kinvara Road. GPS 53.155, -9.080

# MOY HOUSE

**Antoin O'Looney (owner)**
**Brid O'Meara (General Manager)**
**Lahinch, County Clare**
☎ **+353 65 708 2800**
✉ **bomeara@moyhouse.com**
🖰 **www.moyhouse.com**

## Brid O'Meara and her team maintain exactingly high standards in the beautiful Moy House.

Moy House is the real deal. It's handsome, it's distinctive, it's singular. It's a house with a strange sense of mystery. It's a house that unwinds its charms slowly, a quiet, seductive destination that soon captivates you. Here is Eamon Barrett on his visit to Brid O'Meara's house:
'Initially I wasn't sure I liked it. But the more time I spent there, reading, looking out to the rough sea, helping myself to Power's 12-year-old whiskey from the honesty bar, the more I liked it. We had a beautiful room with a built-in window seat and a fabulous bathroom. Lorge chocolates from Kerry were left in the room for us. In the evening, there were slippers and candles. We had our own turf fire in the room, for goodness sake! At breakfast the next morning there was a taste of the level that Moy is pitched at, with truly superb service and an excellent breakfast of scrambled egg with mushroom accompanied by really good brown bread. Staff were excellent - again that all-important welcome from Brid - and nothing we asked for was too much trouble.'
Nothing is too much trouble at Moy House.

- ● **OPEN:** Mar-Dec
- ● **ROOMS:** Nine rooms
- ● **PRICE:** B&B €185-€280 per double room, Suite €270-€360, Single €145-€175

● **NOTES:**
Visa, Mastercard, Laser. Special offers Nov-May. Special packages/group rates available. Dinner, €55.

● **DIRECTIONS:**
Moy House is located about 1.5km south of Lahinch town, on the Miltown Malbay road. Shannon Airport is 45 mins' drive. GPS 52.951381 -9.346285

## SHEEDY'S

**John & Martina Sheedy**
**Lisdoonvarna**
**County Clare**
📞 **+353 65 707 4026**
📧 **info@sheedys.com**
🔗 **www.sheedys.com**

# Martina and John never stop innovating, and their bar food offer is the latest improvement in Sheedy's.

Sheedy's is one of those discreet, modest, family-run hotels that once expressed the hospitality culture of Ireland. Happily, that meticulous, subtle and charming culture of Irish hospitality lives on in this family hotel, thanks to Martina Sheedy's polite, quiet service, and John's delicious cooking. Everything here is done by hand, from the hand-crafted work of their local suppliers to the hands-on care of the kitchen. Sheedy's does things the old-fashioned way. Most recently, John has introduced a series of delicious bar menu dishes, for those who prefer an alternative to the dining room, and the same judicious care is evident in zingy crab claws with garlic butter, or Hereford steak with rocket and Parmesan salad, or crispy duck confit with garlic potatoes, that graces all of their cooking. 'All dishes are cooked fresh to order' it says at the foot of their dinner menu, and that cooked-to-order care extends to breakfast, every part of which is cooked individually. John and Martina Sheedy have to work hard to do this intensive hands-on hospitality, and it is the happy guest who benefits in this pretty and simple hotel.

● **OPEN:** from Easter to early October
● **ROOMS:** Eight rooms and three junior suites
● **PRICE:** €99-€129 per room

● **NOTES:** All major cards accepted. ♿ One room with disabled access. Restaurant open during summer. Bar food available each evening. Special offers available all year, telephone for details.

● **DIRECTIONS:**
200m from the centre of Lisdoonvarna, on the road going out towards the wells.
GPS 53.02771 -9.28909

# VAUGHAN LODGE HOTEL

**Michael & Maria Vaughan**
**Lahinch**
**County Clare**
📞 **+353 65 708 1111**
📧 **info@vaughanlodge.ie**
🖱 **www.vaughanlodge.ie**

## Wealthy golfers and super-fit kite surfers rub shoulders in Vaughan Lodge, captivated by the hospitality.

Multi-millionaire Chip O'Hare, from the United States, stayed at Vaughan Lodge as part of a golfing trip with a bunch of similarly affluent buddies. Kathy Sheridan, of *The Irish Times* asked Chip what he reckoned of Michael and Maria Vaughan's handsome lodgings:

'Vaughan Lodge was excellent', wrote Chip. 'Obviously new and neat and clean. Superb food and service was cordial and first rate. Michael was a great host and hard worker. We had a dinner there on our last night with the guys from Lahinch and it was lovely.'

Well, that's the million-dollar American market taken care of for the foreseeable future, and if you had to bet on a guy to convince those choosy Yanks, then Michael Vaughan would be your banker, your sure bet. He is a consummate hospitality professional, which makes Vaughan's a wonderful place to stay and to eat. Kathy Sheridan also described the sheer effort and dedication it takes from the Vaughans to run a place like this: you know it ain't easy, even if they make it look easy. That's what professionals do. That's what the Vaughans do.

- ● **OPEN:** Apr-Nov
- ● **ROOMS:** 20 rooms, all en suite
- ● **PRICE:** €85-€135 per person sharing. Single €95-€160

- ● **NOTES:** All major cards accepted. ♿ Disabled access. Restaurant, dinner €47. Open 6.30pm-9.15pm Tue-Sat. Private car parking. Loc8 code K20-7303MF

- ● **DIRECTIONS:**
From Ennis, take the N85 to Ennistymon, turn left onto N67 to Lahinch, and the hotel is just inside the 50km zone on the left. GPS 52.933889 -9.341111

# WILD HONEY INN

**Aidan McGrath & Kate Sweeney**
**Kincora Road, Lisdoonvarna**
**County Clare**
📱 **+353 65 707 4300**
✉ **info@wildhoneyinn.com**
🖥 **www.wildhoneyinn.com**

The Wild Honey is simply the perfect destination after a long westward trek to Lisdoon'.

'If you dreamt up the perfect place to tumble into after a long car drive into the western sunset... this would be it', wrote Ms Cleary about Aidan and Kate's fine old coaching inn, a short walk from the square in Lisdoon'.
Indeed, there is something archetypal about the Wild Honey, something enchanting, irresistible. Recently, all five McKennas fell under its spell on a trip down the West coast, and so did Caroline Byrne, and Eamon Barrett, and everyone – everyone! – else we know who has made the trip to Lisdoonvarna. The WHI is on a roll and all the work that Aidan McGrath has done since he first opened Muses in Bunratty, back in 1999, now stands to him: his food is wonderfully poised and exciting, modern yet nuanced with lessons from the past, especially when he uses pickled and fermented vegetables, and makes sublime teases out of quotidian things like lamb neck fillet, or pig's cheek, or shows his complete mastery with fish cookery. The room is as relaxed and enjoyable as the cooking, and we recommend two or three nights – with lots of hiking in between! – to get the full measure of this little beauty.

● **OPEN:** mid Feb-end Dec/early Jan, with restricted opening Oct-Dec/Feb-Apr
● **ROOMS:** 14 rooms, all en suite
● **PRICE:** €40 per person sharing.

● **NOTES:** Visa, Mastercard, Laser. ♿ Disabled access. Restaurant, open 1pm-3.30pm, 5pm-9pm in season, dinner price €32

● **DIRECTIONS:**
From Ennis, take the N18 to Ennistymon. Take the N67 towards Lisdoonvarna, Wild Honey Inn is on your right at the edge of town.

# BALLINTERRY HOUSE
**Michael Garvey & Ann O'Sullivan**
**Rathcormac**
**Fermoy**
**North Cork**
📱 **+ 353 25 87835**
✉ **ballinterryhouse@yahoo.co.uk**

*Something new*

## Ann and Michael's work on Ballinterry House has created a North Cork star.

A relaxing night away at Ballinterry House starts when you pick up the phone, says Caroline Hennessy. A last-minute booking? Seven-month-old baby in tow? Needing supper included? That's fine. No problem. Nothing phases owner Ann O'Sullivan and, after seeing what an enormous labour-of-love restoration job that she and partner Michael Garvey have done on this gracious Queen Anne house, you can understand why. With the remains of a Norman keep standing proud on the way in, a picturesque wood (hazed with masses of bluebells when we visited) just above the house and rows of raised veggie beds outside the window, this recently opened spot is well on its way to having a picture-perfect setting. Inside, three elegant bedrooms are spacious and thoughtfully appointed, ipod docks sitting happily on antiques of yesteryear, a tray armed with sloe gin and pistachios to quell any pre-dinner pangs. Simple home-cooked food is the order of the day here, and Ann makes good use of the well-thumbed array of cookbooks in her kitchen. We felt like lords of the manor. Renovated, renewed – and so very, very relaxing.

- ● **OPEN:** all year, except Christmas
- ● **ROOMS:** Three rooms, all en suite
- ● **PRICE:** €110-€150 per room

- ● **NOTES:** Visa, Mastercard, Laser.
  ♿ No Disabled access
  Supper available on request.

- ● **DIRECTIONS:**
  Just outside the village of Rathcormac, about 200m on the R628 towards Conna, Tallow & Castlelyons

# BALLYMALOE HOUSE

**The Allen family**
**Shanagarry, Midleton**
**East Cork**

📱 **+353 21-465 2531**
📧 **res@ballymaloe.ie**
🖐 **www.ballymaloe.ie**

## Almost 50 years since Ballymaloe House first opened, it's as spry as ever.

'A recent meal at Ballymaloe House was one that could have been served two or three decades ago', says Joe McNamee. 'There is no notion whatsoever of keeping abreast of the latest trends in cooking. And it suffered not one little bit for that thinking: another wonderful meal, in a house where they just keep doing a magnificent job of what they do so simply and so so well.'

Just so, Joe. And when we look back over menus from Ballymaloe that stretch back for almost 25 years, the timelessness of this cooking is ingrained: in 1993 we ate poached salmon with hollandaise, buttered cucumbers and sea kale: in 2005 we ate Gubbeen ham braised in Chablis and cream with piquant beetroot; in 1989 we ate fresh plaice with mushrooms and tomatoes for breakfast; in 2012 we enjoyed the feast that is the Sunday evening dinner buffet; in 2000 we ate sirloin of Cloyne beef with horseradish mayonnaise, fondant potato and roast garlic. After our first visit, we wrote that 'They intend that every detail of each and every aspect is to be as good as it possibly can be, and they succeed in that'. Amen to that.

● **OPEN:** All year, apart from Christmas & two weeks in Jan.

● **ROOMS:** 30 rooms. No suites

● **PRICE:** B&B €80-€125 per person sharing. Single €105-€124

● **NOTES:** All major cards accepted. Dinner 7pm-9.30pm, €70 (buffet dinner on Sun night, 7.30pm). Children welcome. ♿Two disabled-friendly bedrooms.

● **DIRECTIONS:**
From Cork take N25 to exit for Whitegate R630, follow signs for R629.  GPS -8.074930 W 51.865310 N

# BALLYVOLANE HOUSE

**Justin & Jenny Green**
**Castlelyons, Fermoy**
**North Cork**
📱 **+353 25 36349**
📧 **info@ballyvolanehouse.ie**
🖥 **www.ballyvolanehouse.ie**

## Justin and Jenny's iconic Ballyvolane is one of the best-loved destinations.

'We still rear saddleback pigs, we have a smoker in which we smoke fish and meat, we have a house forager, my dad continues to grow a vast amount of vegetables and fruit and we continue to carefully source our ingredients from the local area', writes Justin Green, So, if you ever asked yourself just how Justin and Jenny manage to weave such a wondrous spell in the brilliant and beautiful Ballyvolane, now you know: they work hard, but they are also a couple who are way ahead of the curve. A cutting-edge country house may sound like a contradiction, but not here. Mr and Mrs Green understand exactly how to give a destination just exactly the feeling, the ambience, the fiction, the dream, that you want the house to have, whether you are here for the weekend, for a wedding, or for glamping in a glam Bell tent. This means that Ballyvolane feels exactly the way you want a country house to feel: timeless, pristine, cultured, sheerly beautiful, welcoming, hospitable, friendly, out of time. Ballyvolane House is simply superb, and offers one of the greatest country house experiences you can enjoy anywhere in the world.

● **OPEN:** 1 Jan-23 Dec
● **ROOMS:** Six rooms, all en suite. 'Glamping' in the gardens available May-Sept
● **PRICE:** B&B €75-€115 per person sharing. Single €125-€135
● **NOTES:** Visa, Mastercard, Laser, Amex. Dinner 8pm, €50, communal table. Children welcome. Self-catering also available. Pet friendly.
● **DIRECTIONS:**
From the N8, south just after Rathcormac, take the turn to Midleton and look for the sign for the house. GPS 51.096822 -7.530917

# BLINDGATE HOUSE

**Maeve Coakley**
**Blindgate, Kinsale**
**West Cork**

📞 +353 21 477 7858
📧 info@blindgatehouse.com
🖰 www.blindgatehouse.com

## A beautifully designed and decorated house, Blindgate is run with winning style and verve by Maeve Coakley.

We have always loved the style of Maeve Coakley's house, and the fact that its rather conventional exterior hides one of the most superbly designed and executed interiors of any house in this entire book.

But style doesn't win out over comfort in Blindgate, and so this is a very cosy and very comfortable house to hang out in, and not one of those design traps that involves you suffering for someone else's art. As such, Blindgate is a terrific base for staying, relaxing and exploring, enjoying all the best of Kinsale whilst just being far enough up the hill to ensure peace and quiet when the town is at full tilt, but also allowing you to head out both eastwards and westwards through County Cork to sample the incredible varieties and temptations of the county, both geographically and gastronomically. Maeve's breakfasts are just as stylish and fine as the design, setting you up for the perfect day. The fashion designer John Rocha operates by the maxim that 'If you get the design right at the start, you don't need to change it later'. Ms Coakley's Blindgate House shows how to do just that. It's ageless.

● **OPEN:** Mar-Dec
● **ROOMS:** 11 rooms (seven twin rooms, three standard double rooms & one superior double)
● **PRICE:** B&B €100-€160 per room

● **NOTES:** Visa, Mastercard. No dinner.
♿ Disabled access with assistance, but no walk-in showers. Enclosed parking.

● **DIRECTIONS:**
200m past St Multose Church – just up the hill from the Kinsale Gourmet Store.
GPS 51.703842 -8.5253852

# FORTVIEW HOUSE

**Violet O'Connell**
**Gurtyowen, Toormore**
**Goleen, West Cork**
📱 **+353 28 35324**
📧 **fortviewhousegoleen@eircom.net**
🖰 **www.fortviewhousegoleen.com**

## You need to reach for the superlatives to describe Violet's Cork farmhouse.

'The archetype Irish B&B in all its wonder', says Eamon Barrett, our Ireland-trotting editor, going all Jungian on us for a moment as he describes Violet O'Connell's house in deepest West Cork, hard by the road as you get close to the little hamlet of Goleen, just a stone's throw from the Atlantic Ocean, shadowed by rolling hills to the house's rere.

'The MOST friendly welcome, the MOST impressive breakfast you will ever come across. A warren of comfortable rooms, and the most wonderful care. Probably the best B&B we have ever stayed in. Violet O'Connell is one of the nicest people you will ever meet and we loved every minute staying in this smashing house.'

Mr Barrett's reaction to Fortview is typical, and this is a house that renders the traditional McKennas' Guide editor's reserve utterly redundant: everyone from the McKennas' Guides, and everyone else who has ever stayed here, simply falls in love with this house. Stay for a single night, and you too will fall in love with a unique destination. None of us can resist archetypes.

- ● **OPEN:** 1 Apr-1 Oct
- ● **ROOMS:** Three rooms, all en suite
- ● **PRICE:** B&B €50 per person sharing

- ● **NOTES:** No credit cards accepted. Dinner strictly by prior arrangement only, €35. Two self-catering houses available. ♿ No disabled access. Enclosed car park. Children over 6yrs welcome in house (all ages welcome for self-catering).

## ● **DIRECTIONS:**
Signposted 2km from Toormore on the main Durrus road (R591). GPS 51.539889 -9.640589

## GALLÁN MÓR

**Lorna and Noel Bourke**
**Kealties, Durrus**
**Bantry, West Cork**
📞 + 353 27 62732
📧 hello@gallanmor.com
🖰 www.gallanmor.com

Lorna and Noel's boutique
B&B is a great new
Sheep's Head destination.

Something new

Because we live pretty close to it, we have never actually walked The Sheep's Head Way. So, the challenge of that good 175 kilometre hike remains an ambition, and we think the way to get around to doing it would be to base ourselves in Lorna and Noel's boutique bed and breakfast, the lovely Gallán Mór, and to set out on day trips over the walk each day, set up for the hike by a delicious breakfast. Heck, even if we hadn't such an ambition, then Gallán Mór would simply be a lovely place to get away to. It's a modern, purpose-built house, but the Bourkes have smartly created a new house from the old West Cork architectural vernacular, so it reads new, but feels nice and old. The house is colourful, the rooms are swaddling in their comfort and their crafty utility, and the views out across Dunmanus Bay are eye-wipingly wonderful. You sit up in the house looking out at the waters, feeling on top of the West Cork world – the house seems to sit right in the interior of the landscape it inhabits, thanks to the clever design: the outside brought inside. Families should note that there is a sweet self-catering cottage beside the B&B.

- **OPEN:** All year
- **ROOMS:** Four rooms, all en suite
- **PRICE:** B&B €40-€60 per person sharing,

- **NOTES:** Visa, Mastercard, Laser. No dinner.
♿ One room with disabled access. Self-catering cottage.

- **DIRECTIONS:**
Two miles out of Durrus on the Ahakista Road. Look for their sign one mile after the Brahalish sign, on the right-hand side. GPS N51° 36.578' W9°.35.501'

# GARNISH HOUSE

**Con & Hansi Lucey**
**Western Road, Cork City**
**County Cork**
📱 **+353 21 427 5111**
📧 **info@garnish.ie**
🖱 **www.garnish.ie**

## Garnish is a legendary address in Cork city, thanks to Hansi Lucey's amazing breakfasts, and cosseting care.

Consider this: we were chatting to Hansi Lucey in Garnish House one bright summer's morning a while ago when Hansi suddenly said, in that disarming, sing-song Cork accent: 'You know, but we are having our best ever year in business.'

Mrs Lucey wasn't boasting. She was simply pointing out the strange vagaries of the business, that in a time when the country is broke, and when everyone in the country is either broke or going broke, Garnish House could still be jammers. Full. Busier than ever.

We put her right straight away: if Garnish was having its best-ever year, it was because Hansi Lucey never stops trying to get better, and every one of her team is right there with her, trying to be their best also. Their work, their solicitousness, their skill makes for one of the great Cork city destinations, a place of consummate care and hospitality, a place where the breakfasts are benchmark – sorry, the breakfasts are the stuff of legend – a place where they look after you, from the second you walk in the door to the second you wave goodbye.

- **OPEN:** All year
- **ROOMS:** 30 rooms, including four apartments
- **PRICE:** B&B €38-€52 per person sharing, €59-€80 single, €129 family room

- **NOTES:** All major cards accepted. No dinner. ♿ Limited disabled access. Enclosed car parking. Children welcome.
Self-catering accommodation available.

- **DIRECTIONS:**
Five minutes' walk from the city centre, opposite UCC. GPS 51.8957 -8.4886

41

# GLEBE COUNTRY HOUSE

**Gill Good**
**Ballinadee, Bandon**
**County Cork**
📞 + 353 21 477 8294
✉️ info@glebecountryhouse.com
🖰 www.glebecountryhouse.com

Glebe is a fab country
house and garden in quiet,
lovely West Cork.

*Something new*

The hinterland around Gill Good's beautiful Glebe House, in Ballinadee, is different, entrancing, a little part of West Cork all unto itself. It really struck us how different this zone is when, one afternoon, we were having lunch in Ballinspittle, and a whole crowd of hipster-left-field-alternative types suddenly converged, as if from nowhere. There is an independent, autonomous culture here, and it's delightful, and gives the area its own atmosphere. Snuggling cosily into that away-from-it-all is Ms Good's delightful house and gardens, but Glebe, in fact, is a world-unto-itself, too. There are the gardens, and the gardens furnish the house with lots of things for breakfast and dinner; there are apartments for the entire family to stay; there are the rooms in the house. They cater for weddings, specialise in house parties, and cook delightful food for breakfast and dinner: mushy pea and bacon soup; beetroot quinoa with baby leaf salad; traditional kassler; monkfish in herb hollandaise; rhubarb sponge castles. A confident, sure, hospitable hand is evident in everything in Glebe, so introduce yourself to this very special zone.

● **OPEN:** All year, except Christmas
● **ROOMS:** Four rooms
● **PRICE:** B&B €90 for a double room

● **NOTES:** Visa, Mastercard, Laser. Set menu dinner €35. ♿ No disabled access. Pet friendly. Glebe goodies, fudge, biscuits and home-baking.
Self-catering apartments €260 per week

● **DIRECTIONS:**
2nd house on the right as you come into Ballinadee village from Bandon direction. GPS N51.71197 W008.62855 Loc8 Code WKJ-99-3LN

# THE GLEN

**Diana & Guy Scott**
**Kilbrittain**
**West Cork**

📱 **+353 23 49862**
📧 info@glencountryhouse.com
🖥 www.glencountryhouse.ie

## A beautiful house set in the gorgeous hinterland of Kilbrittain, The Glen is everyway special.

What makes The Glen, Diana and Guy Scott's manor house close to the coast at Kilbrittain, so special? The special nature of the experience of staying here is not simply because of the beauty of the house, although it is very beautiful, or its impressive vintage: it dates from 1860, and is appropriately creeper-clad. It's not even Diana's capacious skills as hostess, at which she is one of the very best we have encountered. No, there is something else going on here, in this beautiful house, which unfolds itself at the end of a long avenue of mature trees, just a stone's throw from the sea. The Glen is one of those places that seem to tap into our need and desire for nostalgia, so there is something fundamentally primal about it. You might have been reared in an elegant Gorbals tenement, but when you step in the door of The Glen you will feel you not only belong here, you will feel you were somehow born here. It's the nostalgia we feel for an imagined, privileged childhood, no matter that a bracing Gorbals childhood is the reality. And that is why The Glen is so special: the inner child is released in this special house.

- **OPEN:** April-Oct
- **ROOMS:** Four rooms and one family unit
- **PRICE:** B&B €60 per person sharing, one night, €55 two nights, €45 three nights.

- **NOTES:** Visa, Mastercard, Laser. No dinner. ♿ No disabled access. Secure car parking. Family unit is for two adults and two children under 16yrs.  Pet friendly.

- **DIRECTIONS:**
Signposted from the R6099 approximately half way between Clonakilty and Kinsale.
GPS 51.533933 -8.700794

# GORT NA NAIN FARM
# VEGETARIAN GUESTHOUSE
Lucy Stewart & Ultan Walsh
Ballyherkin, Nohoval, County Cork

*north*
*east*
*west*
*south*

📱 +353 21 477 0647
✉ lucy@gortnanain.com
🖥 www.gortnanain.com

## Caroline Hennessy's favourite getaway is the unique Gort na Nain, especially thanks to Lucy's amazing cooking.

There they are, on page 18 of Denis Cotter's great cookery book, *For the Love of Food*: 'Lucy's breakfast sausages with spiced tomato chutney'. And don't they look delicious! Who else makes chestnut sausages this good? No one. Just Lucy Stewart.

That's the thing about Gort na Nain: everything looks simple, but everything is sheer class. The hard work is hidden. The comfort of the farmhouse, the cheer of the hosts, the sublime nature of the food, with virtually all of it coming straight from Ultan's acclaimed organic farm. It's their own honey, their own eggs, their own chutneys, breads, pastas, the whole nine yards. So, get your feet under the table with your fellow guests to enjoy baby aubergines stuffed with courgettes and toasted pine nuts; Puy lentil and garlic potatoes wrapped up in chard parcels; home-made rhubarb ripple ice cream. You waft up the stairs to bed and sleep the good sleep and, next morning, there they are: Lucy's legendary chestnut sausages, with a poached egg straight from the happy hens. Ah, the good life was never better than here at Gort na Nain.

● **OPEN:** All year
● **ROOMS:** Three rooms, all en suite
● **PRICE:** €85 for two people sharing, €60 single

● **NOTES:** Vegetarian dinner, for guests only, three courses €30. Bring your own wine. Picnic baskets. Pet friendly (booking essential)
Loc8 Code WBJ-13-SY9

● **DIRECTIONS:**
Take the airport road out of Cork. Turn left at Belgooly. Gort na Nain is five minutes further on up this road. GPS 51.432281 -8.252405

# GOUGANE BARRA HOTEL

**Neil & Katy Lucey**
**Gougane Barra, Macroom**
**County Cork**
📱 **+353 26 47069**
📧 **gouganebarrahotel@eircom.net**
🖱 **www.gouganebarrahotel.com**

## It's Neil and Katy who make Gougane Barra the unique destination hotel it is.

Neil and Katy's Gougane Barra Hotel is one of the nicest hotels in Ireland. If you thought that this sort of family hotel, where she cooks in the kitchen, and where he meets and greets the guests and mans the bar, had vanished under the tsunami of zombie hotels that litter the country, then a trip to the lake of Gougane Barra will restore your soul, your sanity, and your faith in true Irish hospitality. Mrs Lucey's food is pure lovely, a timeless, fashion-free style of unpretentious cooking that fills your heart with joy as it fills your belly with goodness. Mr Lucey is an hotelier of the old school – polite, charming, modest, attentive to every need. We love the simplicity of the rooms, we love walking in the woods, and by the edge of the beautiful, peaceful lake and the church, and one of these days we will bring the rods and see if we can't catch a little fishy in the lake. You don't even need to be a certain age to fall for the magic at work here – Gougane isn't some nostalgia trip, but an entrancing present for your senses. Gougane Barra is priceless, just priceless, the expression of Irish hospitality at its simple, quiet best.

- **OPEN:** early Apr-late Oct
- **ROOMS:** 26 rooms
- **PRICE:** €99 B&B per room

- **NOTES:** All major cards accepted. Theatre by the Lake opens mid July-late Aug. ♿ No disabled access. Restaurant opens breakfast & dinner from 6pm. Special rate for two nights plus one dinner. Sunday lunch.

- **DIRECTIONS:**
Take the R584 between Macroom & Bantry, then the L4643, following signs for Gougane Barra after the Pass. GPS 51°50'20" 09°19'09"

45

# GROVE HOUSE

**Katarina Runske**
**Colla Road, Schull**
**West Cork**
☎ **+353 28 28067**
✉ **info@grovehouseschull.com**
🖰 **www.grovehouseschull.com**

## A West Cork icon, Grove House sits high and handsome on the Colla Road, gazing over the harbour.

'Stayed in Grove House in Schull, which I absolutely love!', writes Eamon Barrett. That's a typical reaction to this lovely Colla Road address, a high and handsone house that looks out over Schull harbour, in deepest West Cork. Katarina Runske is a human dynamo, one of those extraordinary people whose elemental energy is astounding to an outsider. How she does all she does we simply do not know, but she runs the house, the restaurant, the gallery and all else as if it is just an average day's work. Which, to Ms Runske, is just what it is. With her smart young son, Nico, handling things in the kitchen, Ms Runske has moved Grove House centre stage in the hospitality culture of Schull, and Nico is seemingly cut from the same cloth as his Mum: born into the business, he makes it all seem easy, and he is learning at lightning speed, so the cooking here gets better and better with every visit. It's a cliché to say that Grove somehow summarises the classy bohemianism of Schull but, to tell the truth, Grove somehow summarises the classy bohemianism of Schull. It's patrician, eccentric, 100% West Cork, pure lovely.

- **OPEN:** all year
- **ROOMS:** Five double rooms
- **PRICE:** B&B €80 per double room. Single, €50 per room

- **NOTES:** Visa, Laser, Mastercard, Amex. Restaurant open daily in summer, weekends only off season. Dinner always available for guests, from €22.50. Private parking. ♿ No disabled access.

- **DIRECTIONS:**
Take left opposite AIB, turn onto Colla Road, Grove House is about 500 metres on the right-hand side.

# INCHYDONEY ISLAND LODGE & SPA

Des O'Dowd
**Inchydoney, Clonakilty, Co Cork**
📱 **+353 23 8833143**
✆ **reservations@inchydoneyisland.com**
📠 **www.inchydoneyisland.com**

There is ambition aplenty in Inchydoney, and a dedicated team at work.

*Something new*

There is ambition in Inchydoney, and maybe the best way to see it is through this simple portal: in 2012, the student chef of the year competition was won by Shane Deane, an apprentice chef at Inchydoney, who has been working with head chef Adam Medcalfe for the last two years. Strictly speaking, hotel chefs no longer win competitions, which are supposed to be the preserve of young guys and girls working in starred city restaurants. But owner Des O'Dowd and his team are rewriting the book of expectations at this beachside hotel, and they have one of the best, most committed crews working together that we have seen in recent times. On our last visit, we ate splendidly, slept splendidly, and we book-ended our stay with an early-evening swim before dinner in the sea, and then some late morning kayak surfing on the waves of the gorgeous beach. That's the thing about surfing, swimming and kayaking at the hotel: they let you feel immensely virtuous whilst you are merrily indulging all the way, so this is the ultimate feel good. Just make sure to book enough time here to let that sea air and spray get deep into your soul.

- **OPEN:** all year, except Christmas
- **ROOMS:** 67 rooms
- **PRICE:** B&B €95-€125 per person sharing

- **NOTES:** Visa, Laser, Mastercard, Amex.
Gulfstream Restaurant, Dunes Pub & Bistro
Spa, Seawater pool. Self-catering apartments.
♿ Disabled access

- **DIRECTIONS:**
From Clonakilty, follow signs for Inchydoney beach, and the hotel is overlooking the water.

# KILCOLMAN RECTORY

**Sarah Gornall**
**Enniskeane**
**County Cork**

📞 **+353 23 882 2913**
📧 **sarahjgornall@eircom.net**
🖱 **www.kilcolmanrectory.com**

## Straight from the pages of *Country Life*, Sarah Gornall's handsome rectory is simply beautiful.

Sarah Gornall has trained as a chef, she has trained as a gardener, and she has trained as an interior designer, and it's as if all of her education in all of these disciplines has been designed to lead her to create this impeccable house, one of the smartest arrivals on the Irish hospitality scene in recent years.

She is one of those rare people who really can create feng shui by putting the right object in the right place in order to create the right aesthetic: Kilcolman has jumped straight from *The World of Interiors*. 'Sarah Gornall is someone who not only espouses perfection, but somehow makes perfection look easy.' That's how *The Irish Examiner's* Mary Leland summed up Sarah Gornall's modus operandi in this beautiful 19th-century rectory. There is a word – a superb Italian word coined by Baldassare Castiglione in his *The Book of the Courtier* in 1528 – for what Ms Gornall achieves and the way in which she achieves it: sprezzatura: the nonchalance that conceals effort. The effort underscoring every detail in Kilcolman Rectory is huge. You'd never guess.

● **OPEN:** all year
● **ROOMS:** One double/twin en suite, and three double/twins sharing two adjacent shower rooms.
● **PRICE:** B&B €75 per person, sharing. Single €80

● **NOTES:** No credit cards. Dinner €45, advance booking essential.

● **DIRECTIONS:** From Bandon take the Clonakilty road. Turn right after Hosfords Garden Centre. Follow road straight through a crossroads. Carry on until you come to Y junction. Take left fork, and the entrance is third on the right. GPS 51.73128 -8.86649

# HOSPITALITY FAMILIES

**1**

### THE ALLEN FAMILY
### SHANAGARRY, CO CORK

**2**

### THE GREEN FAMILY
### FERMOY, CO CORK

**3**

### THE FOYLE FAMILY
### CLIFDEN, CO GALWAY

**4**

### THE KELLY FAMILY
### ROSSLARE, CO WEXFORD

**5**

### THE MAGUIRE FAMILY
### BLACKLION, CO CAVAN

**6**

### THE O'CALLAGHAN FAMILY
### MALLOW, CO CORK

**7**

### THE O'HARA FAMILY
### RIVERSTOWN, CO SLIGO

**8**

### THE TREACY FAMILY
### KILLARNEY, CO KERRY

**9**

### THE VAUGHAN FAMILY
### LAHINCH, CO CLARE

**10**

### THE WHEELER FAMILY
### RATHMULLAN, CO DONEGAL

# KNOCKEVEN

**John & Pam Mulhaire**
**Rushbrooke, Cobh**
**County Cork**

☎ **+353 21 481 1778**
✉ **info@knockevenhouse.com**
🖱 **www.knockevenhouse.com**

## Afternoon tea in Knockeven House: can you think of anything that could be nicer? No, we can't either.

'The finest traditions of country house hospitality.'
That's what John and Pam Mulhaire promise that you
will experience and enjoy in their gorgeous 1840 manor
house, just outside Cobh. The interesting thing about
their evocation of the tradition of hospitality, however, is
the fact that Pam and John are, relatively speaking, new-
comers at the game, having only opened their house to
guests in 2005. But, however they acquired their mastery
of the tradition, masters of it the Mulhaires most
certainly are. And they are fastidiously innovative, having
added a superb afternoon tea offer in 2012 which quickly
proved to be a big hit with guests. Knockeven is a superb
destination, distinguished by fastidious housekeeping,
characterised by Pam's vivid personality, and galvanised by
her stunningly delicious breakfasts – the scrambled eggs
are amongst the best in Ireland, and her buffet table is a
feast for the eyes, the senses and the appetite. Wrap all
these elements together in this special house, and you
have a place you want to wrap yourself in, savouring every
moment of the tradition of great Irish hospitality.

- **OPEN:** all year, except Christmas
- **ROOMS:** Four double rooms
- **PRICE:** B&B €50-€60 per person sharing. Single
€60-€75

- **NOTES:** Visa, Mastercard, Laser accepted.
♿ No disabled access.  Loc8 W8P -49-MD8

- **DIRECTIONS:**
Leave the N25, turn onto the R624, direction Cobh. Pass
Fota, cross over bridge, take first right. At Great Gas
Motors turn left and it's the first avenue on the right.
GPS 51.848889 -8.318242

# LANCASTER LODGE

Robert White
**Lancaster Quay, Western Road
Cork, County Cork**
📞 **+353 21 425 1125**
📧 **info@lancasterlodge.com**
🖱 **www.lancasterlodge.com**

## Great value, great location and great service means Lancaster ticks the boxes for your Cork city destination.

People are very comfortable in Lancaster Lodge, one of those good, smart, comfortable lodges where you quickly find yourself feeling at home, thanks to amiable, relaxed staff and a very good level of cooking at breakfast. It may sound strange, but when John McKenna stayed here, it kind of reminded him of some campus accommodation, though there are no Jim Fitzpatrick 'Che' posters: just some hi-def American photographic landscapes in groovy colours, and MOMA prints.

What was campus-like about Lancaster Lodge was the laid-back feeling, the ease with which staff and guests re-laxed throughout the house, because certainly the cook-ing has no comparison to college food. The breakfasts are correct and good – good pancakes with bacon and maple syrup; creamed scrambled egg with smoked salmon; a choice of omelettes; and the Full Irish. It's Breakfast's Greatest Hits, and it's all very nicely done, much bet-ter done than one might expect at the very keen prices Lancaster charges. The location is ace, service is good, the place gleams with good housekeeping, and it's a good call.

- **OPEN:** all year
- **ROOMS:** 48 rooms, all en suite
- **PRICE:** B&B €39.50-€69 per person sharing. €86-€119 single

- **NOTES:** All major cards accepted. ♿ Disabled access. 50 parking spaces. WiFi.

- **DIRECTIONS:**
At the bridge, which spans the river on Lancaster Quay, opposite Cafe Paradiso. GPS 51° 53'47"N 8°28'57" W.

# LONGUEVILLE HOUSE
**William & Aisling O'Callaghan**
**Mallow**
**North Cork**
📱 **+353 22-47156**
📧 **info@longuevillehouse.ie**
🖰 **www.longuevillehouse.ie**

## Longueville is virtually self-sufficient, so you will find flavours and textures here that are nowhere else.

There is a voracious element of the pastoral in William O'Callaghan's cooking. Eating in the grand Longueville House, you get the sense that he wants to impart a super-sensory overload of the natural world in his dishes. He can do this, of course, because of his good fortune in having the fruits of Longueville's 500 lush acres to feed his kitchen - everything from salmon to pork to apple brandy to cider to potatoes, all their own, all characterised by true provenance, all characterised and christened by the Longueville terroir, are at his fingertips. But wanting to share this treasure trove is just as much on account of the fact that Mr O'Callaghan is a true countryman: he is an expert mushroom hunter; a fine grower; an orchard keeper; a fish smoker, and his culinary skills take all these ingredients and transform them into a multitude of delightful things for his guests. He tries to bottle the pastoral, does Mr O'Callaghan, he is after its essence, and he takes his ingredients and distils them into sheer deliciousness. You will find flavours and textures and tastes in Longueville House that simply aren't found anywhere else.

● **OPEN:** all year, weekends only Dec-Mar
● **ROOMS:** 20 rooms, all en suite
● **PRICE:** B&B €169-€189 in double room, €209-€239 in junior suite.

● **NOTES:** All major cards accepted. Dinner 6.30pm-8.30pm €55-€90. Recommended for vegetarians. Children welcome. ♿ No facilities for disabled in rooms. Hotel will always open for groups of 20+, half-board.

● **DIRECTIONS:**
5km from Mallow, travelling in direction of Killarney.
GPS 52.133515 -8.720934

# NEWTOWN HOUSE

**Georgie & Michael Penruddock**
**Kinsalebeg, Youghal**
**County Cork**

📞 +353 24 94304
📠 info@stayatnewtown.com
🖰 www.stayatnewtown.com

## 'A true time out', is how Caroline Hennessy describes a day or two at Newtown House, a magical escape.

Caroline Hennessy has described Newtown House as 'a retreat from the hurly burly of life', and capturing that elusive feeling and delivering it explains why guests are so devoted to Georgie and Michael Penruddock's beautiful house, Newtown.

Newtown enjoys a pretty breathtaking location, right on the edge of the Blackwater estuary and directly across from the town of Youghal, so even just arriving here inspires the feeling of escape. Everything that happens thereafter cements the notion that you have gotten away from the real world, you have escaped, you have found a secret hideaway – a big soak in a roll-top bath in the later afternoon, relaxing in front of the fire with a good book, looking out at the birds skimming the estuary, chilling with the newspapers after a delicious breakfast with fruits and vegetables that have just been brought in from the garden, chatting with the Penruddocks about this, that and the other. 'A true time out', says Caroline, and who amongst us doesn't need some true time out every once in a while? Newtown House is the place for a new you.

● **OPEN:** All year
● **ROOMS:** Two rooms, both en suite
● **PRICE:** B&B €65 per person sharing, €100 single occupancy

● **NOTES:** No credit cards.
♿ Limited disabled access. Picnics and light suppers by arrangement.

● **DIRECTIONS:**
From the village of Piltown, turn right to Ferrypoint. Proceed 0.7miles and the entrance is on the right. GPS 51.95911 -7.82313

# PIER HOUSE

**Ann & Pat Hegarty**
**Pier Road**
**Kinsale, West Cork**
☎ **+353 21 477 4475**
✉ **pierhouseaccom@eircom.net**
🖰 **www.pierhousekinsale.com**

## A lovely, stylish house blessed with great hospitality from Ann and Pat, Pier House is an ace Kinsale address.

Is the Pier House a B&B, or a small boutique hotel? You will find it described as both, in different places, and certainly it's a very stylish place if you think in terms of standard B&B design and aesthetics: the Pier is bright, colourful and vivid, unlike so many bed and breakfasts. Then again, it does have those features you might associate with boutique hotels, such as balconies for several of the rooms, and a fine secretive garden, and ice machines for that early evening highball before you head out to town for dinner in a good Kinsale restaurant.

But, truth be told, whatever you choose to call it, what you will remember most about Pier House is not the colourful design, or the luxury specification. What will linger in your memory will be the hospitality of Ann and Pat. Their energy drives this house, their welcome is its secret and its soul, and it sets the house apart from so many other, slick, Kinsale addresses. Mrs Hegarty makes sure everyone is looked after, she cooks lovely breakfasts and maintains a pristine house, and she does it all with charm and relish. The location is simply fantastic.

● **OPEN:** All year, except Christmas
● **ROOMS:** Nine rooms, all en suite
● **PRICE:** €100-€140 per room, including breakfast. Single €80

● **NOTES:**
Visa, Mastercard, Laser. ♿ No disabled access. No dinner. One secure parking space, otherwise public car park right next door.

● **DIRECTIONS:**
Coming from Cork, take first left at SuperValu, left at the tourist office, 50m down on right-hand side.

54

# ROLF'S COUNTRY HOUSE

**Johannes & Frederike Haffner**
**Baltimore Hill**
**Baltimore, West Cork**
📱 **+353 28 20289**
📧 **info@rolfscountryhouse.com**
🖱 **www.rolfscountryhouse.com**

## The proof of how good Rolf's is lies in the fact that the locals eat here. It's a delightful West Cork destination.

Rolf's has come a long way from its early days when it operated primarily as a hostel, and today the accommodation, whilst still simple, is simply lovely: comfortable, cloistered, calm, a beautiful place in which to find yourself at any time of the year.

Happily, the rooms are just as much fun as the cooking you will enjoy in their cosy restaurant, where the true strength is to be found in the Mittel-European specialities that Johannes really savours, such as their stroganoff, for instance, which is as good as you will get anywhere in Europe.

But aside from the comfort, the charm and the spot-on cooking, it is the energy and humour of Johannes and Frederike – and they are witty, droll, animated people – that animates Rolf's and gives it both character and soulfulness, making it a place loved by travellers and, crucially, beloved by locals: Rolf's isn't just for tourists, the locals eat here. It really is a smashing place, whether you are down in Baltimore for the boating, or just wending your way pleasurably through the wonders of West Cork.

- **OPEN:** All year, except Christmas
- **ROOMS:** 14 rooms, all en suite
- **PRICE:** €40-€50 per person sharing, including continental breakfast.

- **NOTES:** Visa, Mastercard, Laser. ♿ No disabled access. Holiday cottages also available. Restaurant open 12.30pm-2.30pm, 6pm-9pm (9.30pm in summer)

- **DIRECTIONS:**
On the way to Baltimore just before village turn sharp left and follow signs, approx 200m up the hill.
GPS 51.480556 -9.367779

# SEA VIEW HOUSE HOTEL

**Kathleen O'Sullivan**
**Ballylickey**
**Bantry, West Cork**
📱 **+353 27-50462**
✉ **info@seaviewhousehotel.com**
🖰 **www.seaviewhousehotel.com**

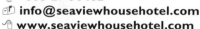

## For very many visitors, Kathleen O'Sullivan's country hotel is one of the greatest Irish hotels.

Hospitality is a conundrum. It has to be unchanging, yet it has to adapt and develop. It has to be personal, and yet it must match the highest international standards. It is best if it is parochial, yet it can't be introverted.

Kathleen O'Sullivan solves all these dilemmas in Sea View House Hotel, a classic Victorian manor house, which has been a home to great Irish hospitality for decades. The way Ms O'Sullivan runs her hotel is the old school way, with correct cooking, correct service, simple and correct design, eager and correct housekeeping. The pleasures to be derived from her didactic approach to running an hotel are myriad. This may be the old school way, but that means it is the good school way, the traditional way, the best way, and this sense of correctness explains why so many customers regard Sea View House as one of their favourite places to stay not just in West Cork, but in all of Ireland. Your heart leaps with anticipation and delight every time you turn up the driveway, and see this elegant house once again, one of the great bastions of unchanging Irish hospitality, run by one of the great hoteliers.

● **OPEN:** mid Mar-mid Nov
● **ROOMS:** 25 rooms
● **PRICE:** B&B Standard €120, mini suite €165 double. Family room for 2 adults & 2 children €150

● **NOTES:** All major cards accepted. Dinner in restaurant 6.45pm, Sun lunch (from Easter Sun) and lounge food daily. Dinner €35-€45. ♿ Disabled access. Secure parking. Pet friendly.

● **DIRECTIONS:**
On the N71 from Cork, 5km from Bantry and 13km from Glengarriff. GPS 51.704722 -9.437222

# SPRINGFORT HALL

**Paul Walsh**
**Mallow**
**County Cork**
📱 **+353 22 21278**
📧 **stay@springfort-hall.com**
🖱 **www.springfort-hall.com**

### Bryan McCarthy is one of the chefs for the future, so get down to Springfort.

*Something new*

Joe McNamee says: 'Bryan McCarthy is establishing a standard for hotel food in the county which is becoming hard to beat. His is a very innovative approach to providing locally-sourced ingredients, with extensive roots in traditional Irish cooking'. Take his twelve-hour feather blade, McCarthy's signature dish, a slow-cooked Hereford beef that melts away on the tongue. This meat, as tender as it is richly umami-flavoured, comes from the school of Advanced Comfort. Actually, a feather blade is one of the cheaper beef cuts, from the shoulder of the animal, and responds best to the gentlest coaxing, the lightest of touches and a large dollop of patience. McCarthy has all that. He also has a sense of adventure, a skittish desire to play around, in this case teaming the beef with an extraordinarily-sweetened swede purée, a savoury, wild three-cornered leek croquette, truffle and beetroot, resulting in a dish to charm all culinary creeds and colours. It is the kind of cooking that is at the heart of the re-invention of Springfort Hall, a delightful country house hotel that is upping its game, big time. A place, and a man, to watch.

● **OPEN:** All year, except Christmas
● **ROOMS:** 49 rooms
● **PRICE:** B&B €55 per person sharing, €65 single

● **NOTES:**
Lime Tree Restaurant dinner €29.95, plus à la carte and early bird. ♿ Disabled access

● **DIRECTIONS:**
Signposted from Newtwopothouse, just south of Buttevant, off the N20 Limerick-Cork road.
GPS -8.66533 52.17962

# WEST CORK HOTEL

**Neil Grant**
**Ilen Street, Skibbereen**
**West Cork**

📱 **+353 28 21277**
📧 **info@westcorkhotel.com**
🖱 **www.westcorkhotel.com**

## Tim, Neil and Aidan power the WCH ever onwards, a dynamic trio bringing a great destination centre stage.

It's one of the happiest stories in contemporary hospitality: two guys leading from the front, and inspiring the rest of their crew, and restoring the reputation of an iconic address. That's the story of what's been happening in The West Cork Hotel, as owner Tim Looney and manager Neil Grant pull this venerable hotel forward. It's hard to know which of these two works the harder, but the net effect of their efforts has been to restore the status of this much-loved hotel: once again, the WCH is a key destination, and a key part of West Cork. It's a great place to stay, with comfy rooms, charming staff and a liberating lack of pretension throughout. Best of all, The West Cork feels like an hotel: it's where you eat, meet, drink, celebrate, debate, enjoy, relax. Everything syncs here – the service, the comfort, the buzz, the charm, the friendliness, and the kitchen team under chef Aidan O'Driscoll is producing some terrific food, not least a Burns' Night dinner that amazed and delighted everyone who enjoyed it. An hotel at the heart of its community, it's a throughly West Cork sort of hotel, the West Cork Hotel.

- **OPEN:** all year, except from 24 Dec-28 Dec
- **ROOMS:** 34 rooms, all en suite
- **PRICE:** B&B €79-€129 per room, €169 per suite

- **NOTES:** All major cards accepted.
Carvery lunch and à la carte dinner in Kennedy's Restaurant. Bar food available all day 12.30pm-9.30pm (closes 9pm off season). ♿ Disabled bedrooms on request.

- **DIRECTIONS:**
At the riverside, on the west side of Skibbereen
GPS 51.550555, -9271061

## CASTLE MURRAY HOUSE HOTEL

**Marguerite Howley**
**Dunkineely, County Donegal**
✆ **+353 74 973 7022**
📧 **info@castlemurray.com**
🖱 **www.castlemurray.com**

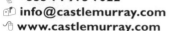

# Castlemurray has been a staple of the McKennas' Guides since forever, a model of consistency and hospitality.

Consistency, credibility, authenticity. That's what you get in Marguerite Howley's Castle Murray House, and this trio of attributes explains why Castle Murray House has been in the McKennas' Guides ever since our first book, written way, way back in 1991, and that is a record held by very few destinations indeed.

Part of Castlemurray's success is explained by the fact that Remy Dupuy has been in the kitchen since 1994, cooking house classics such as prawns and monkfish in garlic butter, tartare of Inver sea trout with blinis, or ravioli of Donegal crab. And, since 1991, we have been writing that the views from the dining room are amongst the most captivating in the entire county, and Donegal is a county that does awesome views to beat the band. The rooms are simple and comfortable, the hospitality is genuine and fetching. 'Peopled by warm, charming staff who made us welcome, made us laugh, and made us some truly excellent food', as a correspondent noted in a fine piece of analysis which explains how Castle Murray works: they make you welcome, they make you happy, you are happy.

● **OPEN:** All year, except Xmas. Weekends only off season. Open 7 days during Jul-Aug
● **ROOMS:** Ten rooms
● **PRICE:** B&B €55-€65 per person

● **NOTES:** Visa, Mastercard, Laser. Restaurant open 6.30pm-9.30pm Mon-Sat; 1.30pm-3.30pm, 6.30pm-8.30pm Sun; Dinner €45. ♿ No disabled access. Pet friendly.

● **DIRECTIONS:**
Castle Murray is signposted just west of Dunkineely.

# THE GLEN HOUSE

**Sonia McGonagle**
**Straid, Clonmany**
**Inishowen, County Donegal**
📱 **+ 353 74 376745**
📧 **glenhouse@hotmail.com**
🖱 **www.glenhouse.ie**

## Sonia McGonagle is a mighty hostess, blessed with boundless energy.

*Something new.*

When Fionn Davenport picked his favourite place to rest his head in the Northwest for the *Defining Ireland* series for Newstalk radio, the place he chose was Sonia McGonagle's The Glen House, in little Clonmany, way up north amidst the stunning natural beauty of the windswept Malin headland.

We understand perfectly.

The Glen is a beautiful house, superbly run by Sonia and her responsive, helpful team, with lovely rooms, with a spick and span tea room you can stop off in after a visit to the Glenevin Waterfall next door. Mrs McGonagle is one of the most meticulous hostesses, with an obsessive attention to detail, whether it is the correct way to place sandwiches and buns and cakes on a cake tier, or how to dress a room, or the standard of housekeeping that makes everyone happy. It is a house that pushes all the buttons, therefore, and we can't think of anything nicer than a few days here, spent walking on the beaches and on through the Urris Hills and the Mamore Gap, with the promise of the return to The Glen to end a perfect day. Ah, Donegal!

- **OPEN:** Mar-Oct
- **ROOMS:** nine rooms
- **PRICE:** B&B €40 per person, sharing

- **NOTES:** Visa, Mastercard, Laser.
Tea rooms open weekends 9.30am-6pm Mar-Jun & Sept-Aug and seven days Jul & Aug. Evening snack menu for guests.

- **DIRECTIONS:**
On the left-hand side just after the entrance to The Glenevin Waterfall Park. GPS 55.267857,-7.436564

# LINSFORT CASTLE

**Alan Rooks**
**Buncrana, County Donegal**
📱 **+353 87 9677244**
**+353 74 936 3148**
✉ **booking@linsfortcastle.com**
🖰 **www.linsfortcastle.com**

*north*
*east*
*west*
*south*

## You never know who you might meet at Linsfort – food writers; Buddhist meditation groups; Reilly the dog.

Alan and Brigeen's Linsfort Castle is a cult destination. Buddhist meditation groups love it. Caroline Byrne loves it: 'I reckon it's possibly the best base for a holiday in Inishowen', says Caroline. 'For starters, Brigeen's gardens, while not only beautiful to walk through, produce fruit, vegetables, free-range eggs (from a clutch of Blackrock hens), and honey, all of which are served up to guests in the B&B. Inside the house, her talented eye is evident in every room, each individually and tastefully decorated, as is every nook of the house. In the old kitchen where breakfast is served every morning, an old fireplace replete with traditional hob and pots, and an old still-working wireless give a certain country elegance.' Like everyone else – Buddhists, Byrnes, McKennas, Hennessys, you name it – Caroline fell under the spell of this charming big house and its larger-than-life hosts. Alan and Brigeen are modest and generous, and they look after you well and cook delicious breakfasts and they introduce you to the riches of this glorious peninsula. Believe us, like everyone else, you simply will not – will not! – want to leave Linsfort.

● **OPEN:** All year
● **ROOMS:** Five rooms, three bathrooms
● **PRICE:** B&B €35 per person

● **NOTES:** No credit cards. Dinner by arrangement. Ideal for small groups or families. Comfortable lounge with library. Sun terrace. Recommended for Vegetarians. Pet friendly. ♿ No disabled access

● **DIRECTIONS:**
Turn left over the bridge on northside of Buncrana. Follow the Inishowen 100 and Dunree road for 4km until road forks. Take left fork. GPS 55.17171 -7.50103

# HOTEL MANAGERS

**1**
**PAUL CARROLL**
**GHAN HOUSE**

**2**
**PATRICIA COUGHLAN**
**NUMBER ONE PERY SQUARE**

**3**
**ANN DOWNEY**
**CONNEMARA COAST**

**4**
**LIAM GRIFFIN**
**MONART**

**5**
**WILLIAM KIRBY**
**MOUNT JULIET**

**6**
**TARA MCCANN**
**THE OLDE POST INN**

**7**
**DONAL MINIHANE**
**HOTEL DOOLIN**

**8**
**FERGUS O'HALLORAN**
**THE TWELVE HOTEL**

**9**
**PATSEY O'KANE**
**BEECH HILL HOUSE HOTEL**

**10**
**PADRAIG TREACY**
**KILLARNEY PARK HOTEL**

# THE MILL RESTAURANT
**Derek & Susan Alcorn**
**Figart, Dunfanaghy**
**North Donegal**

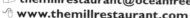

📞 +353 74 913 6985
📧 themillrestaurant@oceanfree.net
🖰 www.themillrestaurant.com

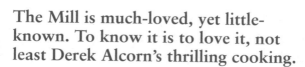

## The Mill is much-loved, yet little-known. To know it is to love it, not least Derek Alcorn's thrilling cooking.

Derek Alcorn is a terrific cook. His food has that great gift of being both earthy and ethereal, and that is a quality few chefs can manage. He juggles the elements of his cooking like a master juggler, all the while distracting your senses with little conjuring tricks – the anchovy beignet with Killybegs seabass; the pickled cucumber with Horn Head crab; the lentil and coriander dahl with scallops (that one is a great Shaun Hill trick, of course); the black pudding bon bons with free-range chicken. It takes some confidence to make bon bons out of black pudding, but if anyone is going to do it, then it is Mr Alcorn. His cooking has grown in both confidence and success over the dozen or more years that he has featured in our guides, and he has the further confidence not to chase any acclaim for his work: he may be the best and least-known chef in the country. He does what he does – he cooks delicious food from cracking ingredients for a devoted and delighted audience, he keeps his bag of tricks fully up-to-date, he encourages his team, he runs a good show, and he makes it all look easy. That may be his greatest trick of them all.

● **OPEN:** Easter to Hallowe'en, weekends off season
● **ROOMS:** Six rooms
● **PRICE:** €50 per person sharing, €75 single.

● **NOTES:** Visa, Mastercard, Laser, Amex.
♿ No disabled access
Recommended for children.

● **DIRECTIONS:**
Dunfanaghy is at the very tip of the country, coming up to Horn Head. From L'Kenny take the N56 through Dunfanaghy. The Mill is 1km past the village on right.
GPS 55.176856 -7.980311

# RATHMULLAN HOUSE

**The Wheeler family**
**Lough Swilly, Rathmullan**
**County Donegal**

📱 **+353 74 915 8188**
📧 **info@rathmullanhouse.com**
🖱 **www.rathmullanhouse.com**

## The Wheeler family are one of the great hospitality tribes of Ireland, gifted with the powers of hospitality.

'Most beguiling of all, there was also an indefinable comfy-ness about the hotel; grand, but lived-in, few airs, but many graces'.

That's Judith Woods, writing in *The Daily Telegraph* about Rathmullan House, and you couldn't sum up the place better than Mrs Woods' fine aphorism: few airs, but many graces. That's Rathmullan alright, a place where the Wheeler family show their dynamic hospitality, their generosity, and their genius for setting the mood of this fabulous house and restaurant at just the right pitch.

You need a few days to get into the swerve of Rathmullan, to slow down to its pace, to get at the level of those many graces. It's a most beloved house, especially for regular visitors from Northern Ireland who adore it and return here often. But the calmness is created simply because the Wheelers work so hard, and there is a continual smorgasbord of events and happenings to divert and delight everyone. Kelan McMicheal's food is set at just the right pitch also, ennobling superb local foods with sympathetic, smart culinary skills. Few airs, many graces.

● **OPEN:** Open all year, apart from mid Jan-mid Feb and closed mid week Nov & Dec
● **ROOMS:** 34 rooms
● **PRICE:** €70-€125 per person

● **NOTES:** Visa, Laser, Mastercard, Amex. ♿ Disabled access Swimming pool. Pet friendly. Family rooms. Loc8 code BNJ-09-X76

● **DIRECTIONS:**
In Rathmullan, turn left at the Mace shop. Go north through the village, past the Blue Church, turn right at black gates. GPS 55.09871 -7.53443

# ABERDEEN LODGE

**Pat Halpin**
**53-55 Park Avenue, Ballsbridge**
**Dublin 4**

📱 **+353 1-283 8155**

📧 reservations@halpinsprivatehotels.com

🖥 www.halpinsprivatehotels.com

A quiet and luxurious
house in leafy Ballsbridge,
Aberdeen Lodge is special.

Every time the McKennas have stayed in Aberdeen Lodge, Pat and Anne Halpin's high and handsome Victorian red brick on leafy Park Avenue in handsome Ballsbridge, we have had nothing but a great time. It's the sort of destination that our kids, who have known Aberdeen Lodge ever since they were wains, love returning to, and it's especially delightful to have such a memorable place to stay in your catalogue of happy childhood memories, a house that is a benchmark for hospitality, for comfort, for great cooking, for chilling, for enjoying whenever it is time to head north from West Cork and visit the Big Smoke.

Aberdeen Lodge works because everything here is done correctly, as it should be and as it has to be, but there is no stuffiness or formality to Pat and Anne, and their professionalism is cloaked in a quiet, modest confidence. The hospitality is primal, the housekeeping is meticulous, the cooking is simply superb, and Aberdeen offers one of the best breakfasts that you can find in the capital, a superb feast to start the day the right way. It's a special place, Aberdeen Lodge. Just ask the McKenna wains.

- **OPEN:** All year
- **ROOMS:** 17 rooms, including two suites
- **PRICE:** €65-€90 per person sharing, €99-€120 single

- **NOTES:** All major cards accepted. Light 'drawing room' menu, €8-€15 per course, extensive wine list. Parking. ♿ Disabled access. Not suitable for children under 7yrs. Concierge service.

- **DIRECTIONS:**
Just down from the Sydney Parade DART station.
GPS 53.325017 -6.213247

# ARIEL HOUSE

**Deirdre McDonald**
**50-54 Lansdowne Road**
**Dublin 4**

☎ **+353 1 668 5512**
✉ **reservations@ariel-house.net**
🖱 **www.ariel-house.net**

For many guests, Ariel is the best townhouse, with the very best breakfast in Dublin city.

A friend who stays regularly at Deirdre McDonald's Ariel House when visiting Dublin put the dilemma in quite simple terms: 'How do you improve on perfection?' Fortunately, he also answered his own question: 'Well, Deirdre McDonald and her team just keep raising the bar and this makes Ariel the best townhouse in the country.' Well, that is about as unequivocal as it gets: the best townhouse in the country.

But, he wasn't finished: 'Ariel also has the best and most consistent breakfast.'

The best townhouse in the country with the best and most consistent breakfast. Okay. We're cool with that. We too love the buzz of Ariel – it's always buzzing! – and we love the breakfast: beautiful baking with brown bread, scones and banana bread; grapefruit with honey and sugar; French toast with crème fraiche and berries; poached eggs and smoked salmon with beurre blanc; a stack of pancakes with maple syrup and grilled bacon. It's all superb: the service is friendly, the house is dramatic, and they are always working to raise the bar even higher.

- **OPEN:** All year, except Christmas
- **ROOMS:** 37 rooms, all en suite
- **PRICE:** B&B from €79 per room

- **NOTES:**
Visa, Mastercard, Laser, Amex. ♿ Disabled access.
Complimentary car parking.
Afternoon tea served 2pm-5pm daily.
Children welcome.

- **DIRECTIONS:**
Right beside the Aviva stadium.
GPS 53.334153 -6.231103

# BROOKS HOTEL

**Anne McKiernan**
**Drury Street**
**Dublin 2**

☎ **+353 1 670 4000**
✉ **reservations@brookshotel.ie**
🖰 **www.brookshotel.ie**

## Few people will disagree that Brooks Hotel is simply the best hotel in Dublin city.

It might seem strange to say it about an hotel, but one of the things that makes Brooks so special – that make it the best hotel in Dublin city, to be frank – is that it has a Mom'n'Pop feel, thanks in particular to manager Anne McKiernan, and chef Patrick McLarnon. Their brilliance gives Brooks an entirely different feel from other city centre addresses. Brooks feels personal, intimate, and real, a place run by people, whereas other places feel they are run by a manual, and consequently feel impersonal, indifferent and unreal. As you would expect of two quietly larger-than-life and surprising characters, the team who work with them are as vivid as the manager and the chef, fascinating characters in their own right, full of stories, full of wisdom. They all sync together perfectly, doing their work with aplomb from the brilliant breakfasts, right through lunch and dinner, and on to a late night whiskey in the bar. Brooks exemplifies the hotel-ness of an hotel, offering not just a welcome, but a real sense of wellbeing. And do take a look at our film portrait of Mr McLarnon, which you will find on the Irish Food Channel on our site.

● **OPEN:** All year including Christmas
● **ROOMS:** 98 bedrooms, including three suites
● **PRICE:** €80-€90 standard double, per person sharing, single supplement €65

● **NOTES:** Visa, Mastercard, Amex. Restaurant open breakfast & dinner. Bar serves food 10am-10pm. Fitness suite. Pillow menu.

● **DIRECTIONS:**
Drury Street is parallel to Grafton St, between Grafton St and Sth Gt George's St, in the centre of Dublin. GPS 53.3421615 -6.2634513

# KELLY'S HOTEL

**Manon Rouel**
**35/37 South Great George's Street**
**Dublin 2**

📞 **+ 353 1 648 0010**
✉ **info@kellysdublin.com**
🖰 **www.kellysdublin.com**

Every city needs a budget
hotel that over-delivers.
Welcome to Kelly's.

*Something new*

How do you make something small look big? How do you
make it look inviting, intimate, cosy, welcoming? How
do you make economy seem expansive, especially when
that economy extends to the amount of money you have
to spend on a project. And how do you make someone
who is travelling economy feel spoiled, special? How do
you make a little seem a lot? In Kelly's Hotel, on Dublin's
South Great George's Street, they manage to make the
pinched seem poetic. The small is made big. The eco-
nomic squeeze is made to seem like a sure fit. You are a
budget traveller, in tycoon territory. You only need one
thing, of course, to achieve all this. And that one thing is
imagination. If you have a little spatial awareness, so much
the better. And a sense of humour, a sense of irony and
history, will allow you to bring it all home, gas in the tank.
Kelly's Hotel does this, and does it brilliantly. They have
made all the smart choices, so the rooms are tiny, but
feel special, bumper. It's a pretty brilliant concept, and the
staff are as cool as the concept – polite, welcoming, nice.
Did we have a great time at Kelly's? We had a great time.

● **OPEN:** All year, except Christmas
● **ROOMS:** 16 rooms, all en suite
● **PRICE:** B&B from €155 per room

● **NOTES:**
Visa, Mastercard, Laser. ♿ No disabled access. Breakfast in L'Gueuleton Restaurant adjacent.

● **DIRECTIONS:**
At the junction where South Great George's St meets
Fade Street, in Dublin city centre.

# NUMBER 31

**Noel Conroy**
**31 Lower Leeson Street**
**Dublin 4**
📠 **+ 353 1 676 5011**
📧 **info@number31.ie**
🖱 **www.number31.ie**

## Do you want to be James Bond, or Henry James? Number 31 can accommodate all your fantasies.

Noel Conroy's house has to be the strangest double act in Dublin's hospitality history.

One half is an ultra-modernist mews, and one half is a classic, traditional Georgian townhouse; it is utterly unique. That it all works, indeed the fact that there seems to be no tension between the two divergent halves of the house, is down to the attention to detail that has been lavished on each room –The Georgians are appositely Georgian, muted and restrained and dignified, whilst the modernists are unapologetically modern, colourful and brutalist – and it helps also that the team here are just as cool as the house itself. They produce one of the very best breakfasts in the city – *The Daily Telegraph* once called the Number 31 breakfasts 'the talk of the town', which is stretching it a bit, but not stretching it too much. Best of all, it's a house that always feels new and alive, no matter how many times you have stayed here, no matter how many new people you have met in the 'conversation pit' drawing room. Number 31 is a classic: classic design, classic house, a classic experience every time you stay.

- **OPEN:** all year, including Christmas
- **ROOMS:** 21 bedrooms
- **PRICE:** €140-€220 per room

- **NOTES:**
Visa, Mastercard, Laser, Amex
♿ No disabled access

- **DIRECTIONS:**
At the upper end of Lower Leeson Street, near the corner with Fitzwilliam Place, in the centre of Dublin.

69

# PEMBROKE TOWNHOUSE

**Fiona Teehan**
**90 Pembroke Road, Ballsbridge**
**Dublin 4**

📞 **+353 1 660 0277**
✉ **info@pembroketownhouse.ie**
🖰 **www.pembroketownhouse.ie**

Fiona Teehan's house is a real peach of a place to stay, a city classic in Ballsbridge.

A beautiful location on tree-lined Pembroke Road is just one of the major assets of Fiona Teehan's Pembroke House. More importantly, the exceptionally fine staff manage to trump the fine location, and in doing so they bring alive the grandeur of this lovely Georgian house. Pembroke is a real peach of a place to stay.
Inside, the bedrooms are calming and very, very comfortable, stylish without being enslaved to design, so their focus is on a comfort that makes you feel very good indeed, especially when the staff arrive with some tea and hand-made biscuits to calm the weary traveller. That feel-good factor is a key element of Pembroke House, because it's one of those elements that is hard to capture, hard to conjure, hard to create. But when someone gets it – as Ms Teehan and her team do – then it means that the guest is a very happy person indeed. They have worked assiduously over the last year and more to make their breakfasts something special, giving the house yet another attraction, and the staff look after you properly, in that waggish Dublin way which is so fine, just so fine.

● **OPEN:** All year, except four weeks at Christmas
● **ROOMS:** 48 rooms, all en suite (incl seven suites)
● **PRICE:** from €99 per room

● **NOTES:** All major cards accepted. Parking complimentary for residents. Car park entrance is on Baggot Lane. ♿ Disabled access.

● **DIRECTIONS:**
Pembroke Road is at the southern end of Upper Baggot Street. Pembroke Townhouse faces Raglan Road with large lanterns on each side of the front door.
GPS 53.332476 -6.23806

# ANGLER'S RETURN

**Lynn Hill**
**Toombeola, Roundstone**
**Connemara, County Galway**
📠 **+ 353 95 31091**
📧 **info@anglersreturn.com**
🖱 **www.anglersreturn.com**

## The Angler's is a house of 'silent sounds', says Lynn Hill. That's the Connemara slang for 'silent music'.

Lynn Hill's Angler's Return is a little bit like Kelly's Resort Hotel, in Rosslare. 'To really enjoy the "real" feel of this house,' Lynn says, 'and to truly relax, one needs three days' stay here, in order to unwind. So many guests suggested this to me last summer, and the ones who stayed a week or more were the happiest, believe it or not!'

We can believe it. Angler's Return, like Kelly's Hotel, is a house that you need to lower yourself into, as if it were a beautiful, big, bubble bath. Just staying one night, and then heading on and rushing through Connemara, is madness personified. You have to let this place into your soul. Angler's Return, says Lynn, is 'a house of peace and silent sounds'. Silent sounds! And silent music.

And when you do that, when you get Zen, you suddenly see the birds, and hear the bees – especially if you are lying on a rug in the pretty garden. And then there is a cracking fire in the evening time in the sitting room, looking out at the lakes and the sunset and maybe a simple, delicious dinner cooked by Lynn. Now, isn't that the real Connemara!? You will surely never be the same again.

● **OPEN:** open Feb-Nov
● **ROOMS:** five rooms, one en suite, four other rooms share two adjacent bathrooms
● **PRICE:** from €90 per double room

● **NOTES:**
No credit cards.
Not suitable for children under 8 years, babes in arms welcome.

● **DIRECTIONS:**
Four miles, on the Galway side, of Roundstone.

71

# BALLYNAHINCH CASTLE

**Patrick O'Flaherty**
**Ballinafad, Recess, Connemara**
**County Galway**
📞 +353 95 31006
📧 bhinch@iol.ie
🌐 www.ballynahinch-castle.com

## Patrick O'Flaherty and his team work endlessly to improve Ballynahinch.

Sam, PJ and John McKenna really had a feast of local Connemara foods on their trip to Ballynahinch. There was slow-cooked McGeough's pork neck in air-dried ham; there was galantine of duck foie gras and confit duck leg; tomato and ginger soup; raspberry sorbet; a quite brilliant assiette of McGeough's Irish pork; and McGeough's beef fillet; lovely black sole cooked on the bone; pecan pie and vanilla ice cream. It was all delicious, proof of Xin Sun's excellence as a cook, and his smartness in sourcing his meats from James McGeough of Oughterard, one of Ireland's best butchers. Breakfast-time, meanwhile, offered a superb buffet table and beautifully cooked food, and the dining room is always a special place in which to enjoy such peachy cooking. Good judgement and excellent staff are the keys to Ballynahinch, as well as a jaw-dropping estate which is essentially a world-unto-itself. The river wends through the estate, and whilst you can't step into the same river twice, you can step into the same Ballynahinch Castle twice, for it is constant, unchanging, faithfully excellent: a Connemara classic in every way.

● **OPEN:** All year, except Feb and Christmas
● **ROOMS:** 40 rooms, including three suites
● **PRICE:** €80-€245 per person sharing, single supplement €40

● **NOTES:** All major cards accepted. Dinner in restaurant, €60. ♿ No disabled access. Private fishery, walking routes and hikes.

● **DIRECTIONS:**
From Galway, take signs for Clifden (N59). At Recess you will begin to see their signs.
GPS N53°27'613 W9°51'787

# ON THE COAST

### 1
**INCHYDONEY ISLAND LODGE & SPA**
**COUNTY CORK**

### 2
**GALLÁN MÓR**
**COUNTY CORK**

### 3
**GROVE HOUSE**
**COUNTY CORK**

### 4
**HOTEL DOOLIN**
**COUNTY CLARE**

### 5
**THE MILL RESTAURANT**
**COUNTY DONEGAL**

### 6
**MOUNT VERNON**
**COUNTY CLARE**

### 7
**PIER HOUSE**
**COUNTY CORK**

### 8
**RATHMULLAN HOUSE**
**COUNTY DONEGAL**

### 9
**RENVYLE HOUSE**
**COUNTY GALWAY**

### 10
**ROLF'S COUNTRY HOUSE**
**COUNTY CORK**

# CONNEMARA COAST HOTEL

**Ann Downey (General Manager)**
**Furbo, Galway**
**County Galway**
☎ + 353 91 592108
✉ info@connemaracoast.ie
🖱 www.connemaracoast.ie

## The period from blink moment to bliss moment takes the merest nano-second in the Connemara Coast Hotel.

Charles Synnott is one of those hoteliers who understands the Blink Moment. He knows that his hotel has to charm and capture you all in the space of a nano-second. But it can't do this with Bling: it has to do it with Bliss, with that ability to make you feel that walking in the doors of the Connemara Coast is just like walking into your home, except your home never looked so fine. You simply have to walk in the door, see the gleam and sparkle, view the ocean glinting through the glass, hear someone greet you warmly, and the Blink Moment is complete, and you say to yourself "How long are we staying!" Your shoulders relax, and time stops. That beautiful feeling – the essence of hospitality; the essence of welcome; the essence of Irishness – is one of the nicest experiences any traveller can have, and the crew in the Connemara Coast Hotel understand it implicitly: it is in their blood, in their modus operandi, in their behaviour. And the team then look after you in a style that congratulates that first moment, serving lovely food, making sure you have what you need, whenever you need it. Blink to bliss, just like that.

- **OPEN:** open all year except Christmas
- **ROOMS:** 141 rooms, standard, superior & executive
- **PRICE:** €89-€125 per person sharing. Supplements (around €50) apply to superior rooms and suites.

- **NOTES:** Visa, Mastercard, Laser, Amex. Mid-week offers available. ♿ Disabled access. Two restaurants, cocktail bar and pub.

- **DIRECTIONS:**
From Galway, follow signs for Clifden and Oughterard. Follow signs to Spiddal and Coast Road, then driving through Barna you will see their sign on the left.

# 7 CROSS STREET

**Olivia O'Reilly**
**7 Cross Street, Galway**
**County Galway**
📞 **+353 91 530100**
📠 **info@7crossstreet.com**
🖥 **www.7crossstreet.com**

## A tiny hotel with intimate rooms right in the centre of Galway city, 7 Cross Street delivers the Galway magic.

Paris has lots of little hotels where you walk through a single narrow door, then down a narrow entrance to a little reception desk and, having checked in, you climb steep stairs to the warren of little bedrooms.

If you are lucky, you have a view of the Parisian skyline. If you don't, you console yourself with the thought that you are still smack in the city centre. Olivia O'Reilly's No 7 Cross Street is one of those Parisian hotels – the narrow doorway on the street, the narrow hall, the tiny reception space, the tiny rooms, the city centre location, the bustle and noise – and it brought back to us floods of memories of staying in inexpensive Parisian hotels when we used to backpack. Happily, it's a Parisian hotel in Galway. So, No 7 suits us perfectly, and if you like petite rooms – let's call them intimate – and cheek-by-jowl eating, then you will love this chic little space on Cross Street. It would be impossible to be more central in Galway city – if you don't fancy the noise, they also have a fine house on Nun's Island you can rent – but we love the at-the-heart-of-the-city feeling, that true, irresistible Galway chutzpah.

- ● **OPEN:** open all year
- ● **ROOMS:** 10 rooms, all en suite
- ● **PRICE:** €65-€99 per person sharing.

- ● **NOTES:** Visa, Mastercard, Laser. Not suitable for young children. ♿ No disabled access due to development restrictions. Parking available 3 minutes' away at reduced overnight rate. Self-service breakfast.

- ● **DIRECTIONS:**
In the very centre of Galway city, Cross Street runs from the main pedestrian walk way High Street, and the Town House is adjacent to Neachtain's Pub.

## DELPHI LODGE

**Peter Mantle**
**Leenane, Connemara**
**County Galway**
📱 **+353 95 42222**
📧 **res@delphilodge.ie**
🖐 **www.delphilodge.ie**

# Peter Mantle and his team have carved out a unique niche amongst the great Irish country houses.

The reason Peter Mantle's country house and estate is world-renowned is not just because of what it is, but also because of what it is not.

Yes, it is an especially beautiful house in one of the most beautiful places in Ireland – if indeed not one of the most beautiful places in the world. And yes it is beloved of fishermen hoping and praying for a salmon to come their way. And it is beloved of food lovers, who relish the creative and ingenious cooking, whilst wine buffs can lose the run of themselves in the incredible selection of wines on the list. But these things alone don't explain Delphi's renown, for equally important to its capacious assets is the fact that Delphi doesn't try to be an hotel, or to ape hotel-style service. It has stubbornly and determinedly set its face against the modern blandness that people think of as luxury. So, instead it is quaint, a place that is comfortable with itself, which means you will be comfortable with it too. In Delphi they know what they can do best, and their best is what they do. It's a simple thing, but it demands a quiet, mighty confidence.

● **OPEN:** Mar-Sep (house parties 18+ off season)
● **ROOMS:** 12 rooms, all en suite (seven with lake view)
● **PRICE:** from €115 per person, sharing, B&B.

● **NOTES:** Visa & Mastercard. Dinner, 8pm, communal table €55. ♿ Disabled access, but not fully disabled-friendly. Flyfishing. Not suitable for children.

● **DIRECTIONS:**
12km northwest of Leenane on the Louisburgh road. In woods on left about half mile after the Adventure Spa. GPS 53.631916 -9.747190

# DOLPHIN BEACH

**The Foyle family**
**Lower Sky Road, Clifden**
**Connemara, County Galway**
📱 **+ 353 95 21204**
📠 **stay@dolphinbeachhouse.com**
🖱 **www.dolphinbeachhouse.com**

## All of the wild magic of Connemara seems to have been collected, collated and distilled in Dolphin Beach.

'Dolphin Beach embodies all I would wish to have in a small hotel', says Elizabeth Field. 'Gorgeous views over the Atlantic Ocean, Slyne Head and Ballyconneely Bay; sparkling clear Western light and fresh breezes; relaxing peace and quiet; wonderful locally sourced food and inimitable Irish hospitality.' Wait, there's more...

'The small details are all there: the comforting pot of tea and biscuits when you arrive; perfect beds with crisp linen; beautiful books to leaf through in the front room; home-made breads and jam. I love the spare, Scandinavian modern decor: lots of wood, lots of windows, rooms that open directly onto a patio.' Wait, there's more...

'Clodagh Foyle has innkeeping in her blood and it shows. She effortlessly juggles a million household tasks and is always ready with a smile. A brief meander up Sky Road after a summer dinner gave us but the baaaah of sheep, the rustling of trees, the smell of honeysuckle and a drawn-out sunset over the water. This is the place I would choose to truly unwind.'

In Dolphin Beach, you get all the magic of Connemara.

- ● **OPEN:** mid Mar-mid Nov
- ● **ROOMS:** Nine en suite rooms
- ● **PRICE:** €50-€75 per person sharing. Single supplement €20

- ● **NOTES:**
Dinner if booked in advance, €37. Visa, Mastercard, Laser. ♿ Limited Disabled access.

- ● **DIRECTIONS:**
Take the Sky road out of Clifden, take the lower fork for 1 mile. It's the house on the sea side.
GPS 53.497778 -10.094722 Loc8 Code is KLR-90-R66

# THE HERON'S REST

**Sorcha Mulloy**
**16a Longwalk, Spanish Arch**
**Galway, County Galway**
📱 **+353 86 337 9343**
✉ **theheronsrest@gmail.com**
🖰 **www.theheronsrest.com**

## 'We loved the breakfast, and Sorcha's super-high energy', says Elizabeth Field.

There actually is a heron, you know, who likes to rest right outside Sorcha Mulloy's riverside house at the Spanish Arch. He's called Jack, and we took a picture of him one time we stayed, in the afternoon just as we arrived at the house. He's photogenic, and patient, happy to stand still long enough so we could get the picture on our 'phone. And once we had the picture, we thought to ourselves: 'Only in Galway'. The rest of the country is littered with houses called Sea View (no view of the sea), Orchard Grove (no orchard, no grove), Chez Nous (wrong country). But, in Galway, Heron's Rest means just that: the place where the heron – Jack – comes to rest. You couldn't make it up. Mind you, you could hardly make Sorcha Mulloy up, either. There is no more meticulous hostess in Ireland. But she's funky, too, and she creates a breakfast that has no parallel in Ireland. Ms Mulloy is actually a highly qualified expert on nutrition, so her breakfasts are not just unique and delicious, they are also powerhouses of health. Elizabeth Field described the Heron's breakfast as 'incredible'. Yeah, incredible it is.

● **OPEN:** 1 May-31 Oct
● **ROOMS:** Three double rooms, two singles: double rooms en suite or private bath, single sharing bathroom.
● **PRICE:** €65-€80 per person sharing

● **NOTES:**
All major credit cards accepted. ♿ No disabled access Street parking in front of house. Children welcome.

● **DIRECTIONS:**
Follow signs for East Galway and Docks. Turn left at the Limerick Steamhouse and follow the road around to the right. Heron's Rest is facing the water.

# INIS MEÁIN SUITES

**Ruairí & Marie-Therese de Blácam**
**Inis Meain, Aran Islands**
**County Galway**
📱 **+ 353 86 826 6026**
📧 **post@inismeain.com**
🖱 **www.inismeain.com**

There is no other place to stay and eat that is anything like the unique Inis Meain.

'Virtual perfection' was the phrase Leslie Williams used to describe dinner in Ruairi and Marie-Therese's Inis Meain Suites. Leslie ate tuna tartare 'virtually jumped off the plate with freshness' – then john dory with shaved fennel, olive oil and chilli – 'the best john dory I have ever eaten'. And when he had gotten a taste of the island potatoes Ruairi and Marie-Therese grow themselves, 'We ate every one and vowed to come back in the summer to taste the new crop'. Everything was perfect: the lobster Américaine with its gentle swaddling of cream, brandy and lobster stock; fresh crab with aioli 'tasted like it came out of the sea an hour before and, here's the thing, it probably did'. Vanilla carrageen mousse with Galway honey was sublime, brown sugar meringues with blueberries, strawberries and mint was 'sophisticated yet incredibly simple'. What it all brought back home to Leslie was 'a sense of place', but the English language isn't really nuanced enough to describe the emotion, so Leslie had to dip into the Irish: tuiscint d'ait 'which is perhaps better because it implies a full and comprehensive understanding'. Perfect.

● **OPEN:** April-Sept
● **ROOMS:** four large suites
● **PRICE:** B&B €250-€350 per person. Two-night stay minimum. Packages available.

● **NOTES:** Visa, Mastercard, Laser. Restaurant open for Dinner, main courses €12-€35.

● **DIRECTIONS:**
Take ferry from Rosaveal, or plane from Inverin.  The Restaurant & Suites are in the middle of the island, pass the only pub on your right, take the next right, then after 100m look out for the stone building on your left.

# KILMURVEY HOUSE

**Treasa & Bertie Joyce**
**Kilmurvey Bay, Inis Mór**
**Aran Islands, County Galway**
📱 **+353 99 61218**
📧 **kilmurveyhouse@eircom.net**
🖱 **www.kilmurveyhouse.com**

## The secret to Aran is to take your time, to let it get into your soul. Kilmurvey House will take you there.

Most visitors to the Aran Islands make a disastrous mistake: they don't stay on the island. Instead, they arrive on the morning ferry, scoot around the island on a bike or in a minibus – don't get us started about how reckless those minibus drivers are, or what damage they do to the island! – and then they leave on an afternoon ferry. Aran Islands done! Did I remember to post my postcard? Next?!
That's not how you do Aran. To understand these mystical islands requires one thing: it requires you to stop. For at least two days, and four days is even better. So, book yourself into Treasa and Bertie's lovely house. Swim in Kilmurvey Bay. Trek the island to see the stones and flowers and waves and colours. Explore Dun Aengus. Relax in the bars of Kilronan. Enjoy Treasa's stupendous breakfasts, amongst the nicest you will ever eat. Enjoy Bertie's hospitality. Borrow a bike and cycle slowly – slowly! – around the perimeter of Inis Mor. Now you are getting it, now you get it. Now it's got you.
Aran has to sink into your soul, and that takes the correct portal. Kilmurvey House is your portal for that pleasure.

● **OPEN:** 1 Apr-16 Oct
● **ROOMS:** 12 rooms, all en suite (seven family rooms)
● **PRICE:** €45-€50 per person sharing. Single €60-€65

● **NOTES:**
♿ No disabled access. Dinner by arrangement only. Complimentary bus to Kilronan for dinner, or evening snack menu served in the house.

● **DIRECTIONS:**
The house is a further 7km from the ferry port. On arrival, take any one of the tour buses.
80

# LOUGH INAGH LODGE

**Maura O'Connor**
**Recess, Connemara**
**County Galway**
📱 **+353 95 34706**
📧 **info@inagh.ie**
🌐 **www.loughinaghlodgehotel.ie**

## Maura O'Connor and her team master the small things in Lough Inagh.

*Something new*

'Sometimes it's the really small things that are memorable', a friend wrote about an afternoon pause at Maura O'Connor's pretty hotel, 'an unplanned stop-over on a long journey that just revitalised us'.

So, what was it in Maura O'Connor's calm, genteel hotel, nestled in the valley on the road from Recess to Kylemore, abutted by the Garroman, Derryclare, Inagh and Kylemore lakes, that was so special?

'The warmth of service, welcoming and quietly confident, yet attentive and eager to please, the fact that they may have been doing this for years, yet every visitor is unique and important.'

Now, there is the rub, and there is the kernel and the secret and the raison d'etre of Lough Inagh: every visitor, even those just dropping in for a cup of tea 'is unique and important'. So, hike the roads, hike the hills, fish the loughs, and come back here and let them make you feel 'unique and important'. And then a fine dinner, a great night's sleep, and tomorrow do it all again. Lough Inagh is delightful, a special place, a place for the small things.

● **OPEN:** Mar-Dec
● **ROOMS:** 13 rooms
● **PRICE:** from €130 per room, €198 dinner, B&B

● **NOTES:**
All major credit cards accepted. Dinner, €44. Hill walking, fly fishing, cycling available.

● **DIRECTIONS:**
Take N59 from Galway as far as Recess. Turn right to R344 signed Letterfrack and Lough Inagh Fishery. GPS 53.51990 -9.74213

# THE QUAY HOUSE

**Paddy & Julia Foyle**
**Beach Road, Clifden**
**Connemara, County Galway**
☎ **+353 95 21369**
✉ **res@thequayhouse.com**
🖰 **www.thequayhouse.com**

## Elizabeth Field got Paddy and Julia Foyle just right: 'funny, warm, urbane and welcoming'.

Elizabeth Field's reaction to Paddy and Julia Foyle's gorgeous house articulates every duality that makes this house extra-special: peaceful yet dynamic; stylish yet relaxed; private yet public, a world apart.

'This place has tons of style: overstuffed sofas and chairs, walls chock-a-block with paintings and ornaments; plump pillows; meandering corridors. Our room on the third floor overlooked the quay. It was HUGE, with a canopy bed, comfortable seating, and I think a fireplace. Also a lovely old-fashioned large bathroom. The breakfast was outstanding: scrambled eggs with smoked salmon; porridge with berry compote; and all the fixings of the full Irish, something I really miss on the other side of the pond. The Foyles are absolutely dynamic: funny, warm, urbane and welcoming. It's a 3-minute walk to town, which is quite nice, as the town can get pretty crowded. So you feel like you're in your own private, rambling, wisteria-covered residence. I wouldn't want to stay anyplace else in Clifden.'

And you won't want to stay anyplace else, either.

● **OPEN:** mid Mar-early Nov
● **ROOMS:** 14 en suite rooms, including rooms with kitchens
● **PRICE:** B&B from €67.50 per person sharing, €85 single rate

● **NOTES:**  Visa, Mastercard, Laser. No dinner.
♿ Disabled access. Street parking.

● **DIRECTIONS:**
The Quay House is down on the quays, past the small playground, and overlooking the harbour.
GPS 53.463525 -10.033264

# RENVYLE HOUSE

**Ronnie Counihan**
**Renvyle, Connemara**
**County Galway**
☎ **+353 95 43511**
✉ **info@renvyle.com**
🖰 **www.renvyle.com**

## A masterly manager and a masterly chef give Renvyle its cutting-edge.

Ronnie and Tim, manager and chef of Renvyle House, are one of the great double acts in Irish hospitality and food. Between them, Mr Ronnie Counihan and Mr Tim O'Sullivan have created a manifesto for Renvyle that is one of the most compelling examples of contemporary Irish ingenuity. It means that Renvyle looks like an hotel and has the scale of an hotel, but feels more like a country house. It means that the food is cutting edge, and yet is also simple and unpretentious, earthy and agrestic, smartly sourced from excellent local artisan suppliers.
It means that Renvyle feels traditional, and has the patina and charm of tradition, yet it is just as modern as you need it to be. Reconciling all these seeming contradictions takes a particular form of genius, and these two genial blokes have it in spades. Genial geniuses seems just the right way to describe them, and this beautiful house is fortunate to have two guys who so completely understand it and appreciate it, and are thereby able to present it at its best to guests. There is no more soulful, relaxing place in the west of Ireland than beautiful Renvyle.

● **OPEN:** Mar-Nov. Open for Christmas.
● **ROOMS:** 70 rooms
● **PRICE:** B&B €40-€120 per person. No single supplement. Look out for offers on website.

● **NOTES:** All major cards accepted. Restaurant dinner, 7pm-9pm, €50. Seasonal outdoor heated swimming pool and golf. ♿ Disabled access. Pet friendly.

● **DIRECTIONS:**
The hotel is signposted from Kylemore. At Letterfrack, turn right, and travel 6.5km to hotel gates.
GPS 53.609167 -9.999167

83

# SEA MIST HOUSE

**Sheila Griffin**
**Clifden, Connemara**
**County Galway**
☎ **+353 95 21441**
✉ **sheila@seamisthouse.com**
🖰 **www.seamisthouse.com**

## Sheila Griffin's bed and breakfast is bohemian and blissful, and vividly different in its own delightful way.

A stone-clad, handsome house dating from the 1820's, set just down the seaward road off the main square in Clifden, Sheila Griffin's Sea Mist bed and breakfast is one of those houses that define the essence of McKennas' Guides. How do you do that? How do you clock up the list of details that means you earn entry into a book like this? Well, one of the signifiers we look for is people who are happy to be different. So, at Sea View, there are no televisions in the bedrooms. Sheila Griffin takes the opposite point of view from those who think every room has to have a flat screen TV along with a stereo and wi-fi and whatnot. Ms Griffin knows that if you are in Connemara, you should be out on the Twelve Bens, or at least enjoying her lovely garden, or relaxing in the aesthetic of her beautiful house. So, she does things differently, and we like that. Just as we like the fact that she cooks with imagination and makes the most scrummy breakfasts, and graces her house with a cool bohemian ambience that flows directly from her own vivid personality. The courage to be different: that's what Ms Griffin has, that's what we seek.

- **OPEN:** Mar-Nov
- **ROOMS:** Four rooms, all en suite
- **PRICE:** €40-€60 per person sharing, single supplement €15-€25

- **NOTES:** Visa, Mastercard, Laser, Amex. No dinner. ♿ No disabled access. No facilities for children. Limited enclosed parking.

- **DIRECTIONS:**
Beside the Bank of Ireland, a little away from the town centre. Sat Nav 53.4882 -10.0244.

# THE TWELVE HOTEL

**Fergus O'Halloran**
**Barna Village,**
**County Galway**
📱 **+ 353 91 597000**
📠 **enquire@thetwelvehotel.ie**
🖱 **www.thetwelvehotel.ie**

## Fergus O'Halloran heads up a terrific team in the funky Twelve Hotel.

*Something new*

The Twelve, a groovy, colourful hotel at the junction in Barna, west of Galway city, is a fascinating place. It's as modern as all-get-out and yet… and yet, it's actually utterly traditional, and it is utterly traditional in a uniquely Irish way. How so? It's simple. It's because of the team who work with manager Fergus O'Halloran, who work in the old Irish way, which is to say: they look after you. They are patient, funny, generous, and unself-conscious. They make the experience of staying here utterly special and, in the bar and restaurant (and their fabulous pizzeria), you see this social genius at work at pell-mell pace: Barna, New York. Barna, Tokyo. Barna, San Francisco. A key player in their success, alongside the brilliant management team, is chef Martin O'Donnell. Mr O'Donnell is a sure-handed cook – and, take note, a keen forager on the local shoreline – and he is an ambitious chef, and his cooking matches the colourful, modern palette of the hotel – Marty's mussels with baby mussel fritters; Connemara seatrout with poached oyster; scallops with McGeough's smoked sausages. Lovely food, lovely place.

● **OPEN:** all year
● **ROOMS:** 48 rooms and suites
● **PRICE:** from €79-€130 per room. Suites also available.

● **NOTES:** Visa, Mastercard, Laser, Amex.
The Pins Bar Bistro, Pizza Dozzina, shop and bakery. Children welcome. Enclosed parking.

● **DIRECTIONS:**
On the main street in Barna.

# BROOK LANE HOTEL

**Dermot & Una Brennan**
**Kenmare**
**County Kerry**
📱 **+353 64 664 2077**
📧 **info@brooklanehotel.com**
🖥 **www.brooklanehotel.com**

## The lovely Brook Lane is an elegant and funky little boutique getaway, superbly run by Una and Dermot.

Dermot and Una Brennan are like the late Steve Jobs: they tweak, endlessly, endlessly, seeking to improve everything they do. Whether it's in the comfy, cosy confines of the Brook Lane Hotel, or in the intimate collation of rooms in No 35, their hip restaurant in the centre of Kenmare, just a couple of minutes' walk from the hotel itself, they are always looking for ways to get better.

Like Mr Jobs, they scarcely need to tweak, for they have a habit of getting things right from the outset. But they are restless hoteliers, and intensely self-critical, so they worry about the breakfast in the hotel – it's great, so don't miss their breads, and the brilliant Sneem black pudding – and the food in Casey's Bistro – don't miss the signature chowder and the signature gourmet burger – and the menu in No 35 – don't miss the incredibly funky pizzas. It's the happy customer who benefits from all this tweaking, however, and the Brook Lane is one of those happy places that just get better and better. As you would expect, the staff are superb, the rooms are comfortable, and we love the intimate, cosy scale of the hotel.

● **OPEN:** Open all year, except Christmas
● **ROOMS:** 20 rooms, all en suite.
● **PRICE:** B&B from €130-€195 per room, €90 single. €210-€290 per suite.

● **NOTES:** Visa, Access, Mastercard, Laser. Casey's Bistro open lunch and dinner. ♿ Disabled access. Private parking.

● **DIRECTIONS:**
Just outside Kenmare, on the right-hand side, at the beginning of the Ring of Kerry, going towards Sneem. GPS 5153.013N 935.4655W

# CASTLEWOOD HOUSE

**Helen & Brian Heaton**
**Dingle**
**County Kerry**
📱 **+353 66 915 2788**
✉ **castlewoodhouse@eircom.net**
🖰 **www.castlewooddingle.com**

## Brian and Helen's breakfasts are a legend, but they are only one element of the professionalism in Castlewood.

Castlewood is the sort of destination that Irish tourism needs in abundance. Brian and Helen Heaton run the house like the utter professionals they are, always playing to their strengths and, in particular, creating a breakfast offer that is one of the very best in the country, executed with a stunning precision that gladdens the heart every morning. Castlewood is one of the great breakfasts.

But the Heatons also make sure that despite being so busy – and they continue to enjoy success, despite everything going on with the Irish and European economies – that they have time to chat, to offer local knowledge, to make sure that you are in the know, to make sure that you have what you need, even if you aren't entirely sure just what it is that you need. Don't worry: they know.

Style; comfort; service. Yes, you get all these at Castlewood but, above all, there is an intimacy about staying in a house like Castlewood which means that you feel you are right at the centre of the action, even if you are actually at the water's edge of Dingle Bay. It's a house that is a hub for hospitality, and for good times, for the best times.

- **OPEN:** Feb-Dec. Open over New Year.
- **ROOMS:** 12 rooms, all en suite.
- **PRICE:** B&B from €45-€95

- **NOTES:** Visa, Access, Mastercard, Laser.
No dinner, but plenty of local restaurants within walking distance. ♿ Disabled access, elevator.

- **DIRECTIONS:**
From Dingle take R559 towards Slea Head river. House is just 5 minutes' walk from marina and aquarium.
GPS 52.141311 -10.286142

# HEATON'S

**Nuala & Cameron Heaton**
**The Wood, Dingle**
**County Kerry**
📱 **+353 66 915 2288**
📧 **heatons@iol.ie**
🖱 **www.heatonsdingle.com**

## Dingle is advancing its case to be the true culinary capital of Ireland. So head to Heaton's to sample the action.

McKennas' Guide editor Caroline Byrne perfectly captured the singular element that makes Heaton's special, when she wrote that 'Cameron and Nuala kept a constant presence should we ever have needed anything, and any request was instantly obliged'.

That's the secret of Heaton's, and what makes it one of the best destinations in beautiful Dingle. It's that constant presence, that awareness of their guests and their guests' needs, that mind-reading quality that the best people in hospitality seem to have as part of their DNA.

Heaton's is a fine, modern, comfortable house, a short walk from the bustle of the town and with fine views out over the bay. Above all, it's a destination where the owners go the extra mile for their guests, preparing the most sublime breakfasts, and with the added bonus of David Heaton, a chef who has earned considerable experience in many of Ireland's best restaurants before returning home, rattling the pans in the kitchen. Dingle these days is a fun, self-confident and diverse getaway, and Heaton's is your base for getting a taste of all that Dingle action.

- **OPEN:** all year, except Dec-Feb. Open New Year.
- **ROOMS:** 16 rooms
- **PRICE:** €40-€65 per person, €46-€75 deluxe room, €54-€85 junior suite.

- **NOTES:**
Visa, Mastercard, Laser. ♿ Disabled access. Children welcome

- **DIRECTIONS:**
Overlooking the Harbour, just down from the Marina, near the roundabout in the centre of Dingle.
GPS 52.140594 -10.113581

# HOTEL EUROPE

**Michael Brennan**
**Fossa, Killarney**
**County Kerry**

north

east

west

south

📱 **+353 64 667 1300**
📧 **reservations@theeurope.com**
🖱 **www.theeurope.com**

## The Hotel Europe doesn't render people speechless when they recall its delights. It renders them monosyllabic.

The Hotel Europe renders people monosyllabic. Ask them what they thought about their stay at this grand, de-luxe destination on the lake's edge in Killarney, and you get a monosyllabic response: 'Bliss'.

Anything else? Oh yes, Alex Nahe's cooking is smart and hip and his ingredients are impeccably sourced. And the rooms are amazing, and the views from the rooms are even more amazing. And the staff are fantastic. But, then they get back to where they were: 'Bliss. It was bliss'.

The bliss is no accident. As Eamon Barrett has pointed out, such luxury would be empty without the appropriate levels of commitment and service to animate it, and here the Europe comes good: 'The staff are excellent... and there is a sense that, whatever your request, the Europe will be able to fulfil it'.

We have mentioned before two especially superlative elements of the Europe, the spa and pool, which are all their own work, and the views across the lake from the hotel, which are the work of Mother Nature, at her very best. Get a taste of these, and you'll fall in love with Killarney.

- **OPEN:** Feb-Dec
- **ROOMS:** 187 rooms and suites, all en suite.
- **PRICE:** B&B from €110 per person sharing

- **NOTES:** All major cards accepted. ♿ Disabled access. ESPA Spa, swimming pool, tennis, horse riding, fishing and many other activities available. Panorama Restaurant, Brasserie Bar, Spa Café, Lounge service.

- **DIRECTIONS:**
Just outside city centre, take the N72, travelling in the direction of Killorglin you will see sign on left.
GPS 52.067033 -9.571089

# THE KILLARNEY PARK HOTEL

**Padraig & Janet Treacy**
**Kenmare Place, Killarney**
**County Kerry**

☎ +353 64 663 5555
✉ info@killarneyparkhotel.ie
🖱 www.killarneyparkhotel.ie

## We can still recall the first time we ever stayed at the Killarney Park.

Padraig and Janet Treacy own two other hotels in Killarney: the boutique The Ross and the grand The Malton, along with the Killarney Park. The Ross is one of our favourite boutique hotels, whilst The Malton is grand and traditional. Caroline Byrne says: 'I couldn't fault The Malton, it was superb. I love that they've kept it very old-world and not just the usual bland modern stuff. They served terrific food throughout the event (Ms Byrne was working!), breakfast, lunch and dinner, and my room was superb… I was sorry to have to leave it!'

That's the Treacy signature: you will indeed be sorry to leave these great temples of hospitality, temples of great cooking, temples of comfort. The Treacys are obsessive about getting the details right, and their staff follow them to the letter. If we were to choose just a single element of the KP to show you how obsessive they are, then it would be the housekeeping: this hotel gleams like few others. But then, we could also choose the cooking, which is superb, and the service, which is superb, and the spa, which is superb. The Killarney Park is one of the world's best.

● **OPEN:** All year, except Christmas
● **ROOMS:** 68 rooms
● **PRICE:** €250-€450 per room and suites

● **NOTES:** Visa, Mastercard, Amex, Laser. Restaurant & Bar, Dinner €55. Children welcome. ♿ Disabled access. Swimming pool, spa.

● **DIRECTIONS:**
At 1st roundabout in Killarney (coming from Cork), take 1st exit for town centre. At 2nd roundabout take 2nd exit and at 3rd roundabout take 1st exit.
GPS 52.0647 -9.5142

# QC'S

**Kate & Andrew Cooke**
**Cahersiveen, Ring of Kerry**
**County Kerry**
📱 +353 66 947 2244
📧 andrew@qcbar.com
🖱 www.qcbar.com

## A mix of superb cooking in the restaurant and comfortable, colourful rooms makes QC's a Kerry star.

The five rooms in Kate and Andrew Cooke's restaurant with rooms, Q.C's, are the grooviest in all of Kerry. Killarney's The Ross comes close when it comes to style, to panache, but the use of colour here, the shocks of colour of the throws and the headboards against the calm colours of the walls and the wood, interplayed with the control of light through shutters and Velux windows, is an utter triumph. You don't just want to stay in these rooms, you want to possess them, such is their astute luxury, their beyond-good finishing, their sense of escape. One of the secrets of their success may be that the rooms and furnishings are slightly larger-than-normal-life – there is space for lying, lounging, bathing, sleeping, dreaming, sharing breakfast in the room. God dammit, you can even stretch out and do your pilates and tai chi. So, we want to walk the Kerry Way around Cahersiveen, then return here each evening for baths and then a scrummy dinner of ace seafood in the restaurant, where Frank Bruni of *The New York Times* raved about the brilliant fish cookery. If it's good enough for Frank, it's good enough for us.

● **OPEN:** All year, open Mon-Sun Easter-Oct, open weekends only off season
● **ROOMS:** Five rooms, all en suite
● **PRICE:** €90 per room

● **NOTES:** Visa, Mastercard, Laser. Restaurant open lunch & dinner Easter-Oct, weekends only off season, Dinner €45. ♿ Disabled access.

● **DIRECTIONS:**
In the centre of Cahersiveen, which is on the Ring of Kerry. GPS 51 56.753 North, 10 13.620 West

# THE ROSS

**Ciara Treacy**
**Town Centre, Killarney**
**County Kerry**
📞 **+353 64 663 1855**
✉ **info@theross.ie**
🖰 **www.theross.ie**

## Ciara Treacy's uber-hip boutique hotel is ahead of the curve, with great rooms, drinks, food and service.

A new generation of the Treacy dynasty are taking up the reins at the family's iconic Killarney destinations. Ciara Treacy is now running the show in the super-stylish The Ross, the hotel where her grandmother first established the Treacy reputation as hoteliers par excellence, beginning a tradition that has been continued by her dad, Padraig, who runs both The Killarney Park and The Malton, but who served his time here in the centre of town, learning the business. The Treacy signature is the art of being ahead of the curve, so The Ross not only has the slickest style in town, but also has the best cocktails in town, a vital signifier in an area where Irish hotel bars have lagged behind the international trend to hire talented mixologists to give their bar an identity. So, a strawberry daiquiri for Mrs McKenna and a whiskey sour for Mr McKenna and then downstairs for dinner in Cellar One, where the cooking is as colourful and hip as the hotel's singular design ethos – chicken schnitzel with pesto; cod with soy mustard; Kerry beef with tomato and chorizo ragout. The Ross is impossibly cool, and that's why we like it.

- **OPEN:** All year, except Christmas
- **ROOMS:** 29 rooms and suites
- **PRICE:** B&B €190-€220 per room and suite

- **NOTES:**
All major credit cards accepted.  Restaurant open for breakfast & dinner. Bar lunch. Wheelchair access. Private car parking. Leisure facilities at the Killarney Park.

- **DIRECTIONS:**
In the centre of Killarney, just round the corner from the main high street, beside the church.
GPS 52.05782 -9.50811

# SHELBURNE LODGE

**Tom & Maura Foley O'Connell
Killowen, Cork Road, Kenmare
County Kerry**

📱 **+353 64 664 1013**
📧 **shelburnekenmare@eircom.net**
🖱 **www.shelburnelodge.com**

## Maura Foley has given more to Irish hospitality than anyone else we know.

Back in 1961, Maura Foley opened a cake shop in Kenmare. She didn't have a mixer, but that didn't stop her. In 1991, she opened Packie's restaurant. In the mid 1990's, she began to renovate and develop Shelburne Lodge, which first appeared in the McKennas' Guides in 1997. Baker. Chef. Hostess. Mrs Foley can do it all. Has any other Irish person had such a major impact on the food culture of an Irish town? The answer, we would say, is: no. Mrs Foley's standards have set the template for Kenmare for more than half a century. Whilst many consider Myrtle Allen of Ballymaloe House to be the originator of contemporary Irish cooking, since opening up Ballymaloe in 1964, Mrs Foley was actually there a few years before. Her achievement over more than 50 years is immense: a most distinguished cook, a most distinguished hostess, a most distinguished restaurateur. And Shelburne stands as testament to all her gifts, a most beautiful house characterised by fabulous comfort and design, characterised by great cooking, characterised by spontaneous generosity. Mrs Foley is the one, she's the one and only one.

● **OPEN:** Mar-mid Dec
● **ROOMS:** Seven rooms, all en suite
● **PRICE:** €100-€160 per room. Single €80

● **NOTES:**
Visa, Mastercard, Laser. No restaurant (good restaurants locally). Enclosed car parking. No wheelchair access. Low season special rates available. Children welcome, high chair, cot.

● **DIRECTIONS:**
300m from the centre of Kenmare, across from the golf course on the Cork road.

# THE INN @ BALLILOGUE CLOCHÁN

**Pat McCarthy, Ballilogue, The Rower, Inistioge, County Kilkenny**
📱 + 353 51 423857
✉ enquiry@ballilogueclochan.com
🖰 www.ballilogueclochan.com

### Eamon Barrett would be more than happy to take up residence in the beautiful Inn @ Ballilogue Clochán.

'Nestled away on a boreen near The Rower in South Kilkenny, Pat McCarthy's farmhouse renovation is a star' says Eamon Barrett.

'The Inn is a collection of old outbuildings that have had a magic wand – and not a small amount of money – waved over them to create a series of beautiful rooms, rooms that are both vernacular and cutting edge. Exposed stone walls, old dressers and mismatched crockery are mixed with power showers, Barcelona chairs, original art and lovely light fittings. The manager, Mark, offers tea and lemon cake on arrival and later, while we slip into pretending that we actually live here and read books in one of the lounges, he brings local cheese and oat biscuits to go with a nice bottle of Sauvignon Blanc. The surroundings are sylvan, the garden is perfect, good taste abounds. Next morning the breakfast doesn't miss a beat: fresh orange juice, homemade brown bread, light as a feather pancakes with Greek yoghurt, blueberries and honey, cinnamon French toast with maple syrup. Value is excellent and The Inn @ Ballilogue is simply a stunning achievement.'

● **OPEN:** mid Feb-Halloween and 27 Dec-2 Jan
● **ROOMS:** 6 rooms, all en suite or with private bathroom
● **PRICE:** B&B €120-€195 for two adults sharing
● **NOTES:** Visa, Mastercard, Laser. ♿ Disabled access. Mature gardens. Not suitable for children. Self-catering & pet friendly accommodation available. Cafe open, 1pm-6pm on Bank hols, home-made cakes.
● **DIRECTIONS:**
10km south of Inistioge, direction of New Ross (R700). Look for a sharp right turn signed for Ballilogue (L8293). Travel for 2km, Ballilogue is on your right, wrought-iron gates. GPS 52.43.11 -6.99.21

## MOUNT JULIET

**William Kirby**
**Thomastown**
**County Kilkenny**
📱 **+ 353 56 777 3000**
📧 **info@mountjuliet.ie**
🖱 **www.mountjuliet.ie**

# With a restaurant team that is currently on top of its game, Mount Juliet is a key destination.

'Everything was near-perfection', a friend wrote after enjoying Cormac Rowe's cooking in the elegant Lady Helen restaurant at the elegant Mount Juliet resort. With the great Mijke Jansen heading up the service, Mount Juliet is operating at full steam, and the cooking has a confidence and an élan that is utterly winning. The sort of attention to detail Mr Rowe is achieving is maybe best summed up by Connie McKenna's listing of the colours featured in a single dish of turbot with lentils, heritage carrot, kombu and fennel: Connie found 'sap green; yellow ochre; burnt umber; cadmium yellow; lemon yellow, white, and touches of grey.' And what did John McKenna think? 'Superb'. He's a man of few words.

McKenna used the same adjective to describe the game terrine – 'Superb' – gave multiple positive marks to the delicate pumpkin sorbet, was wowed! by the Knockdrinna Snow, and agreed with his friend that what the two had enjoyed was 'a perfect meal in one of Ireland's most beautiful dining rooms'. Mr Rowe and his team are on a roll right now, and Mount Juliet is simply not to be missed.

● **OPEN:** all year, including Christmas and New Year. Weekends only off season.

● **ROOMS:** 31 rooms, all en suite, 10 lodges and 16 club house rooms

● **PRICE:** B&B €109-€159 per room, with supplements for suites.

● **NOTES:** All major cards accepted. ♿ Disabled access. Equestrian centre, leisure centre, golf course.

● **DIRECTIONS:**
Leave the M9 on exit 9. Drive through Stoneyford and look for their sign. GPS Locate Code RC3-58-KV7

# IVYLEIGH HOUSE

**Dinah & Jerry Campion**
**Bank Place, Portlaoise**
**County Laois**

📱 **+353 57 862 2081**
📧 **info@ivyleigh.com**
🖰 **www.ivyleigh.com**

## Everything in Dinah Campion's house is geared towards the comfort and well-being of the guest: brilliant.

Tradition is one of those terms the Irish aren't really comfortable with. Talk about traditional food, for instance, and they imagine some fossilised culinary relic of times past, rather than a contemporary food culture infused with knowledge of the past.

Similarly, when it comes to design, the Irish reckon you have either got to be modern, or live in an ancient mausoleum, complete with draughts. Dinah Campion's lovely house, Ivyleigh, proves that this dichotomy is false.

The style here is traditional, but is infused with a modern eye that emphasises lightness and brightness. The cooking, at breakfast, is traditional, which is to say it takes the best of the past and shares it with the best of the present – delicious cooking, but modern and light, well-sourced and cooked with exacting precision. And the house is grand, but tempered with modern touches. Mrs Campion, in this way, creates a masterly synthesis in Ivyleigh, making for a place of good-mannered civility, understated charm, an alliance of the personal with the professional that is terrifically successful. Ivyleigh House is the star of Portlaoise.

● **OPEN:** All year, except Christmas
● **ROOMS:** Six rooms, all en suite
● **PRICE:** B&B €40-€75 pps. Single room €55-€85

● **NOTES:**  Visa, Mastercard. No dinner.
♿ No disabled access.
Off-street car parking. available.
Children over 8 years welcome.

● **DIRECTIONS:**
In Portlaoise, follow the sign for multi-storey car park. At car park entrance there is a sign with directions for Ivyleigh House.

96

# ROUNDWOOD HOUSE

**Hannah & Paddy Flynn**
**Mountrath**
**County Laois**
📱 **+353 57 873 2120**
✉ **info@roundwoodhouse.com**
🖰 **www.roundwoodhouse.com**

## A wabi sabi Arcadian country house, Roundwood House is relaxed, friendly and simply terrific fun.

'It's still a family environment and our guests seem to like that', Hannah Kennan told Mary Leland in *The Irish Times*. Thank heavens for family continuity, for new genera- tions who are happily carrying on the pioneering work of their parents. Can you just imagine what would have happened to Roundwood if it had fallen into the hands of some 'developer'. The family environment would have been the first victim of such a change – even though it explains everything – everything! – about this gorgeous house. And that unique character would have been quickly followed by a lavish spend that would have obliterated the very thing that makes Roundwood so lovable – the fact that it isn't polished and perfect, but has, instead, a wabi sabi quality to it. Wabi sabi Roundwood? Well, yes, actual- ly. Roundwood expresses the perfection of imperfection, the beauty of something aged, something organic.
And now, blessed with the energy of Hannah, and her husband Paddy, Roundwood is perfectly poised for the future, with that unique family environment intact, the house is ready for the next 300 years.

● **OPEN:** All year, except Christmas
● **ROOMS:** 10 rooms, all with private bathrooms
● **PRICE:** €60-€80 per person sharing. Single supple- ment €15

● **NOTES:** All major cards accepted. Supper or din- ner available, €35-€50. Book by noon. ♿ No disabled access. Recommended for children.

● **DIRECTIONS:**
Turn right at traffic lights in Mountrath for Ballyfin, then left onto R440. Travel for 5km on the R440.
GPS 53.024 -7.527

# THE MUSTARD SEED

**Daniel Mullane**
**Echo Lodge, Ballingarry**
**County Limerick**
📱 **+353 69 68508**
📧 **mustard@indigo.ie**
🖱 **www.mustardseed.ie**

Aoife Cox describes Dan
Mullane as 'impossibly
gracious and generous'.

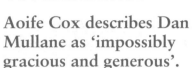

Food writers tend to discuss things such as whether a farmhouse cheese shares the character of its creator, or whether a winemaker makes wines in his or her own image. It's pleasantly ridiculous nonsense, but what they don't do is to devote enough time to the subject of whether or not places to stay have the character of their creators and owners. OK, Aoife Cox, tell us the story of Echo Lodge:"Echo Lodge has just as much personality as Dan Mullane does, and Dan Mullane makes for an impossibly gracious and generous host". So, there you have it: a man and his house, both impossibly gracious, both impossibly generous. That is, indeed, the Dan Mullane we have known for almost twenty five years, a man with a rare passion for hospitality, and man who exhales generosity with every breath. Echo Lodge is one of the great destinations, simply and precisely because Mr Mullane has fashioned a house in his own image, and bequeathed to it his character, his graciousness and generosity. He is a master of design, as well as a master of hospitality, and the result of his gifts, of his work, is simple and straightforward.

- **OPEN:** All year, except last 2 weeks in Jan & Xmas
- **ROOMS:** 18 rooms, including three suites
- **PRICE:** €65-€160 per person

- **NOTES:** Visa, Mastercard, Access. Dinner €62. ♿ Disabled access. Box room special rate €65 per person, sharing. Early bird menu options. Pet friendly.

- **DIRECTIONS:**
Take the Killarney road from Adare, 500m until you reach first turning off to the left, signed for Ballingarry. GPS 52.474672 -8.864692

# NUMBER ONE PERY SQUARE

**Patricia Coughlan**
**1 Pery Square, The Georgian Quarter**
**Limerick City, County Limerick**
☏ **+353 61 402402**
✉ **info@oneperysquare.com**
🖰 **www.oneperysquare.com**

## 'There is nothing average about any of it', is how Aoife Cox describes 1PS.

'I had a wonderful overnight stay in No. One Pery Square in June', says Aoife Cox, 'and I think it very much deserves to retain its spot in the best 100 list. There is nothing average about any of it, from the indoor and outdoor spaces to the food served and the service delivered. It's elegant and tasteful, and everything about the place speaks of wonderful attention to detail. Easily my top pick for Limerick city.'

The world pretty much concurs with Aoife, and we think the most salient part of her critique is the remark that 'There is nothing average about any of it'. That is One Pery's signature – everything Patricia Coughlan and her team do here strives to make every element of the experience real, authentic, enlivening, charismatic, generous, memorable. They are terrified of being average, and yet they manage to be much more than just above average. They manage, in fact, to be unique: few other hotels have a signature style as sharply carved, as strikingly personal, as One Pery Square. So, it's Aoife Cox's first pick for Limerick. And it's everyone's first pick for Limerick.

● **OPEN:** All year, except 24-27 Dec
● **ROOMS:** 20 rooms, all en suite
● **PRICE:** €67.50-€97.50 per person sharing

● **NOTES:** All major credit cards accepted. Dinner available in Brasserie. ♿ Disabled access. Spa and wine shop. Valet car parking. Afteroon tea in drawing room.

● **DIRECTIONS:**
On the corner of Pery Square and Barrington Street.

# VIEWMOUNT HOUSE

**Beryl & James Kearney**
**Dublin Road, Longford**
**County Longford**
☎ **+353 43 334 1919**
📧 **info@viewmounthouse.com**
🖱 **www.viewmounthouse.com**

## Viewmount House is the Longford superstar, with folk from all over Ireland coming to stay and eat.

Viewmount is the place that has put County Longford on the culinary map. Thanks to Beryl and James Kearney's hospitality, and Gary O'Hanlon's dynamic cooking, Longford has gotten the destination it has so long needed. Viewmount itself is a place with two identities: there is the original house, dating from the 1740's, surrounded by peaceful gardens with especially beautiful, mature trees, and this is where James and Beryl Kearney look after you, and make sure you have whatever it is you need.
The second identity, then, is the modern, uber-hip VM restaurant where every Longford food lover – and many food lovers from much further afield – come to eat delicious, inventive cooking from Mr O'Hanlon, cooking which exploits the richness and variety that can be sourced from local artisans, hunted down by Mr O'Hanlon himself. The McKennas all ate superbly when at Viewmount, both at dinner, and with a brilliant breakfast cooked by James, served in one of the atmospheric rooms of the house. It's a mighty one-two, one of the best double-acts in Irish cooking and hospitality.

● **OPEN:** Open all year
● **ROOMS:** 12 rooms, all en suite
● **PRICE:** B&B €55-€65 per person

● **NOTES:** Visa, Mastercard, Laser, American Express. VM Restaurant, Wed-Sat 6.30pm-9.30pm & Sun lunch 1pm-4pm. Lunch €29, Dinner €53. ♿Disabled access.

● **DIRECTIONS:**
From Longford town, take R393 to Ardagh. After 1km take right turn onto slip road and then follow signs to the house. GPS 53.72246 -7.77105

100

## GHAN HOUSE

**Paul Carroll**
**Carlingford**
**County Louth**
📱 **+353 42 937 3682**
📧 **ghanhouse@eircom.net**
🖰 **www.ghanhouse.com**

# Ghan House gets better every year, ageing gracefully, maturing beautifully, a great getaway.

'It feels warm and used'. We're quoting proprietor Paul Carroll on his beloved Ghan House, in Carlingford. That's why, he suggests, brides and bridegrooms pick it for their wedding. That's why business is on a four-year high, with corporate business, weddings and people seeking mid-week value D'n'D's. That's why his car park is full of modest cars with registrations from throughout Ireland, and why accommodation is matching food in the steady increase of business. '95% of my business is from Ireland and the local market is hugely important for us.' Not everyone feels that. One customer complained because 'the furniture is old'. But maybe that was in a time when all our values changed. On the Sunday we stayed both the rooms and the restaurant were busy. We think of it as a place that has seasoned. It has seasoned like your favourite pan, which with careful use only gets better, more useful, more valued. Flowers filled the house, arranged by Joyce, Paul's mother. Ghan is a one-off, like a small, clubby hotel, with an elegant chap at its helm, and a good team. Ghan is a beacon of Irish hospitality, a national treasure.

● **OPEN:** All year, except Christmas & New Year
● **ROOMS:** 12 bedrooms, all en suite
● **PRICE:** €99-€125 per person sharing, includes dinner

● **NOTES:** Visa, Mastercard, Access, Amex. Restaurant open six nights. ♿ No disabled access. Midweek and weekend breaks. Cookery school. Horse riding.

● **DIRECTIONS:**
First driveway on left after 50kph sign on entering Carlingford from south. 85km from Dublin, 69km from Belfast. GPS 54.3990  6.18235

101

# BERVIE

**John & Elizabeth Barrett**
**The Strand, Keel, Achill**
**County Mayo**

☎ **+353 98 43114**
✉ **info@bervie-guesthouse-achill.com**
🖰 **www.bervie-guesthouse-achill.com**

## Bervie is an archetypal seaside house that transforms everyone into a child as soon as they arrive.

Philosophy. Don't you just love a house, a destination, a major address, where the first category on their website – even before you get to the accommodation and the food – is 'philosophy'. Ah, little Bervie, an old coastguard station dating from 1932, a place where you step from the garden through a little wicket gate, and there you are on the beach at Keel Strand. (That sounds like it comes from a children's book, but it is utterly true.) If this is philosophy, then it is epicureanism, pure and simple, the simple and modest life, the untroubled soul, flecked with sea salt and sand and sunshine. Bervie makes you a child all over again. Elizabeth cooks whilst John pulls the corks, and the food, like the philosophy, is simple and true, the foods of the area cooked in the way that suits them best. Don't miss the unique Achill lamb, which enjoys a distinctive pré-salé taste that deserves to have its own geographical label, for it is as distinctive as Connemara lamb, but more saline, more succulent. The food, the comfort, the calm rooms, all chime as sweetly as good philosophy. Bervie creates a synthesis for your soul, a philosophical getaway.

● **OPEN:** Easter-Nov
● **ROOMS:** 14 rooms, all en-suite
● **PRICE:** B&B €50-€65 per person sharing. Weekly, full board rates also available.

● **NOTES:** Visa, Mastercard, Laser.
Dinner available in their restaurant.
Dinner €45. Wine list.
Musical evenings, adjacent beach.

● **DIRECTIONS:**
In the village of Keel on Achill Island.
GPS 53.972686 -10.084319

# KNOCKRANNY HOUSE

**Adrian & Ger Noonan**
**Westport**
**County Mayo**
📱 **+ 353 98 28600**
📧 **info@khh.ie**
🖱 **www.khh.ie**

## The oblique quality of Seamus Commons's cooking is a major part of the thrill of Knockranny House Hotel.

We got a letter from a friend, not so long ago, who had stayed at and eaten at the Knockranny, and who didn't get it. The letter was an interesting corrective to the tsunami of approval and avalanche of accolades that has been the staple diet for Seamus Commons and his team at the hotel. Indeed, you probably have to go back to the glory days of Robbie Millar in Shanks, in the late 1990's, to meet up with a comparable level of admiration to match the acclaim won by Mr Commons. But, we can see how people might not get what Mr Commons does. To borrow a modern phrase, he deals in Obliquity. His food isn't straight ahead (as Robbie Millar's was). Instead, he likes to meander with his ingredients – he will cook skate and add a traditional parsley and garlic persillade, but then there will be a note of lemongrass with the carrot, and black bog potato with a scallop, and a carrot and caper dressing. The food is part-thriller, part-mystery. As Ben Ratliff has written, about the jazz music of David Virelles, 'you might have to contain your need for immediate comprehension'. Get over that little hurdle, and this food will amaze you.

- **OPEN:** All year
- **ROOMS:** 97 rooms, all en suite
- **PRICE:** B&B and dinner from €99

- **NOTES:**  Visa, Mastercard, Amex.
Restaurant open dinner, €54. Bar lunch available.
♿ Disabled access.

- **DIRECTIONS:**
Off the Dublin/Castlebar Road, 5mins from Westport town centre.
GPS 53.80306 -9.50806

# LISLOUGHREY LODGE
**Niall Kerins (General Manager)**
**Cong**
**County Mayo**
📞 + 353 94 954 5400
✉ reception@lisloughreylodge.com
🖰 www.lisloughreylodge.com

*Jonathan Keane's cooking is the jewel in the pretty Lisloughrey Lodge.*

Here's the thing about Lisloughrey Lodge:
Jonathan Keane is a very fine chef, but he is still a chef in development, he is still finding his voice. As Elizabeth Fields points out, he will serve Mulranny sea trout with fennel, apple, mint and peas and the dish will be a dream. He will pull off a great dish of quick-fried scallops with turf-smoked black pudding and there will be a halo of great rustic flavours throughout the dish. But then a nettle risotto with braised beef will have lost its flavour somewhere along the way, and rigatoni with nettles and wild mushrooms will have overcooked pasta. But, you know, that's okay, because these are the mistakes of a young man who is simply trying too hard, trying to do too much as he trawls through his many-coursed menus of discovery. His error is to have a surfeit of ambition, and we applaud that. We only wish some of the hotel staff at Lisloughrey itself shared his ambition to wow! the guests – there are some bodies here that need to be shifted. If you stay, make sure to head down to the lough for a swim: it is bliss incarnate, and sets you up for dinner.

- **OPEN:** All year
- **ROOMS:** 24 bedrooms and 26 suites
- **PRICE:** B&B €140-€220

- **NOTES:** Visa, Mastercard, Amex.
Restaurant open dinner, €54. Bar lunch available.
♿ Disabled access.

- **DIRECTIONS:**
Off the Dublin/Castlebar Road, 5mins from Westport town centre.
GPS 53.80306 -9.50806

# PLACES FOR WALKERS

### 1
**BALLYNAHINCH CASTLE**
**CASTLE WALKS**

### 2
**HOTEL EUROPE**
**THE KERRY WAY**

### 3
**GALLÁN MÓR**
**SHEEP'S HEAD WAY**

### 4
**GHAN HOUSE**
**THE TAIN WAY**

### 5
**THE GLEN HOUSE**
**URRIS HILLS**

### 6
**LOUGH INAGH LODGE**
**RECESS TO KYLEMORE**

### 7
**MULRANNY PARK**
**GREAT WESTERN GREENWAY**

### 8
**RICHMOND HOUSE**
**THE COMERAGH MOUNTAINS**

### 9
**ROUNDWOOD HOUSE**
**SLIEVE BLOOM WAY**

### 10
**STEP HOUSE HOTEL**
**THE BARROW WAY**

# MULRANNY PARK

**Dermot Madigan**
**Mulranny, Westport**
**County Mayo**
☏ **+ 353 98 36 000**
✉ **info@mulrannyparkhotel.ie**
🖱 **www.mulrannyparkhotel.ie**

## Dermot Madigan and his team have been rewriting the Rules For Success manual in the Mulranny Park.

The County Mayo renaissance which has seen so many destinations feature in the various McKennas' Guides in recent years has been one of the most gladdening events in modern Ireland. There is a sense of camaraderie and commitment amongst the chefs, food producers, restaurateurs and hoteliers which is currently unmatched in Ireland, and the Mulranny Park has been at the centre of this renaissance over the last decade. Right from the off, the hotel was setting new standards for hospitality and cooking, and chef Ollie O'Regan has guided the hotel's Nephin Restaurant with a creative, capable culinary signature. The Nephin is a beautiful room – it has the verve and sparkle of Kelly's Hotel and the buzz and atmosphere of Pichet, a pretty potent cocktail of influences even before you have taken your seat. Mr O'Regan's food then drives the pleasure principle home – the cooking is lush, ruddy and comforting as well as technically perfect and expertly balanced, and we would walk to Mulranny for the rack of Nephin lamb with smoked celeriac. Build up your appetite on the Greenway, then satisfy it in The Nephin. Bliss.

● **OPEN:** All year
● **ROOMS:** 41 rooms, all en suite, 20 apartments
● **PRICE:** B&B €55-€85 per person sharing.

● **NOTES:** Visa, Mastercard, Laser.
Nephin Restaurant open dinner, €40 Waterfront Bar menu served noon-9pm. ♿ Disabled access.

● **DIRECTIONS:**
From Westport, take N59 through Newport. Continue on the R311 to Mulranny village. Pass through the village and the hotel is on your right.
GPS 53 54.334, 9 46.908

# STELLA MARIS COUNTRY HOUSE HOTEL

**Frances Kelly & Terence McSweeney**
**Ballycastle, County Mayo**
📱 **+353 96 43322**
📧 **info@StellaMarisIreland.com**
🖰 **www.StellaMarisIreland.com**

## Ten years of sublime cooking and wonderful hospitality from Frances and Terence is the Stella signature.

When we first wrote about Terence McSweeney and Frances Kelly's country house, Stella Maris, way back in 2003 just after they opened, we predicted it would be one of the stars of the next ten years. Everything a great country house needed was in situ, most of all the dynamism of this talented couple. For once – once! – we were right. Stella Maris today, as it celebrates a decade of great hospitality and great cooking, is recognised as one of the best places to eat and stay in Ireland, and it has gained that reputation thanks to the devotion and discipline of this couple, a pair of fastidious hotel keepers if ever there was one. Ms Kelly's cooking, in particular, is all her own, and modestly and precisely executed in every detail. It is food that comforts while it delights, country cooking ennobled by classy ingredients, cooking that has the most complete confidence of all: the confidence to be simple, the confidence to let the food be itself, and to taste of itself. Years after you first eat Ms Kelly's food, the memories of the precise flavours and textures will come back to you, happy memories of the place that is Stella Maris.

● **OPEN:** Easter-early Oct
● **ROOMS:** 11 rooms
● **PRICE:** B&B €95-€120 per person sharing

● **NOTES:** Visa, Mastercard. ♿ Disabled access. Limited ability to accommodate young children. A la carte dinner served 7pm-9pm.

● **DIRECTIONS:**
Go down the hill from Ballycastle, and the Stella Maris is signposted from here. Turn right, it's on the Pier Road, overlooking the sea.
GPS 54.298484 -9.388575

# WESTPORT PLAZA

**John Clesham**
**Castlebar Street, Westport**
**County Mayo**
☎ **+353 98-51166**
✉ **info@westportplazahotel.ie**
🖱 **www.westportplazahotel.ie**

## Westport is on a mighty wave of acclaim these days, and the town deserves every accolade.

Joe and Anne Corcoran's hotel is one of those destinations where things are always done correctly. The greeting, the service, the cooking and the housekeeping all sync beautifully here, and the professionalism of the staff gladdens the heart.

The Corcorans have a very clear vision of creating and keeping a happy workforce as the means by which you create happy guests in an hotel, and they have made this simple, sympathetic philosophy work, both in the Plaza itself and in its larger, adjacent sister hotel, the Castlecourt. There is such an evident sense of commitment from the staff here, that it strikes you the very second you walk through the door – nothing is too much trouble, anything you need to know they know already, or will find out for you just as quickly as they can. This is just the spirit you want to discover when staying in a resort hotel in a holiday town like pretty Westport, and manager John Clesham and his crew come up trumps. Nice cooking in Restaurant Merlot – Angus beef with horseradish mash; Newport lamb with piperade – completes the picture.

- **OPEN:** All year including Christmas
- **ROOMS:** 87 rooms, all en suite
- **PRICE:** B&B €49-€160 per person sharing

- **NOTES:** Visa, Mastercard, Laser, Amex.
♿ Disabled access. King-size beds & Jacuzzi bath in all rooms. Full restaurant facilities in the Restaurant Merlot and Plaza Bar

## ● DIRECTIONS:

As you approach the town from Castlebar the hotel is at the first set of traffic lights on your right-hand side. GPS 53.801261 -9.518608

# COOPERSHILL HOUSE

**Simon O'Hara**
**Riverstown**
**County Sligo**
📱 **+353 71 916 5108**
📧 **reservations@coopershill.com**
🖱 **www.coopershill.com**

## Coopershill is a study in smart, sustainable and elegant country living.

There is something about Coopershill that is artfully smart. You could take one look at this big 18th-century pile and feel sorry for the owners – the maintenance! the heating bills! the roof! the damp!

But your sympathies would be misplaced, for the house is actually uber-green, and has several major environmental awards patting them on the back for their wood-burning stove, for their rainwater harvesting, for their wetland drainage system. They have a tidy business selling their superb venison, another award-winning venture that has developed organically and successfully. And when you stay and eat dinner, they can virtually count how many metres many of the ingredients you will be enjoying will have travelled to reach your plate: 50 metres for the vegetables? 200 metres for the venison? Some of it will be even closer. Country houses used to be worlds unto themselves, and Simon and Christine run Coopershill in just that fashion: self-sufficient people, hard-working people, in a supremely self-sufficient place. It's a gorgeous house, and Christine's cooking is amongst the best country cooking you will find.

● **OPEN:** Apr-Oct B&B, Private groups, minimum 12, all year
● **ROOMS:** Eight rooms, all en suite
● **PRICE:** B&B €99-€122 per person sharing
● **NOTES:** Visa, Mastercard, Laser. Children welcome, tennis court, gardens, croquet, walks. Pets can overnight in owner's car. ♿ No disabled access. Afternoon tea €7, for residents, Picnics €15 pp, light lunch €15, Dinner €49
● **DIRECTIONS:**
On N4, 19km south east of Sligo. At Drumfin crossroads follow signs. GPS 54.1381 -8.4154

# INCH HOUSE
**Mairin Byrne**
**Thurles**
**County Tipperary**
☎ **+353 504 51261/51348**
✉ **mairin@inchhouse.ie**
🖰 **www.inchhouse.ie**

## A quarter century of hospitality and service is the Egan family's contribution to Tipperary.

The Egan family are amongst the most dynamic of the generation of food pioneers who together have created the impressive wave of artisans and restaurateurs that now characterise the county of Tipperary.

John and Nora Egan opened their house to guests in 1989, adding the restaurant five years later, so there is nearly a quarter century of service from the family to their community, to their guests. Whilst Nora Egan has ceded the day-to-day running of the house to her daughter, Mairin, she has developed a parallel career as the creator of Inch House black pudding, a wonderful artisan pudding, which won a bronze award at the Concours International du Meilleur Boudin competition in France in 2011. Mairin, meanwhile, runs this fine house and restaurant with the confidence that comes of family experience, and both the house and the restaurant are places of quiet excellence, a rare quality that we admire enormously. Inch is a wonderfully comfortable place to stay, and a wonderfully comfortable place to have dinner, enjoying the real Tipperary tastes and treats. Don't miss the black pudding!

● **OPEN:** All year, except Christmas
● **ROOMS:** Five rooms, all en suite
● **PRICE:** €45-€55 per person sharing, Single supplement €10. Dinner and B&B offers available.

● **NOTES:**
Visa, Mastercard, Laser. Dinner 6.30pm-9.30pm Tue-Sat. ♿ No disabled access.

● **DIRECTIONS:**
6.4km from Thurles on the Nenagh Road, R498. Turn off at the Thurles exit on the main N8 road.
GPS 52.7211183 -7.92173333

## THE OLD CONVENT

**Dermot & Christine Gannon**
**Clogheen**
**County Tipperary**
📱 **+ 353 52 746 5565**
📧 **info@theoldconvent.ie**
🌐 **www.theoldconvent.ie**

An overnight stay and dinner
in The Old Convent will
recharge anyone's batteries.

Old Convent? New Convent! might be more like it. All
the new things that obsess restaurateurs and food writers
are simply meat and drink to Dermot Gannon. He elides
innovation under his culinary wing as if he were simply
breathing the morning air – sunchoke velouté; goat's curd;
smoked salt; trout caviar; 30-hour pork; bento box dining.
All that stuff you were reading about in *The New York
Times* is actually happening in little – and we mean little –
Clogheen, and it is being used by one of the great modern
cooks to create one of the great modern Irish culinary
signatures. Dinner in the OC is a single, 8-course tasting
menu, and the chef and his team pay tribute to their
county, to their suppliers, and their culinary creed, as the
food unravels a series of dazzling productions. But whilst
Mr Gannon likes to assimilate modern tropes, he always
finds a logic in his dishes – that 30-hour rare-breed pork
will have Highbank syrup rooting it to the orchard the pig
might have grazed in; the Goatsbridge trout caviar will
bring the river to the marine tang of Connemara smoke-
house salmon. Fabulous food, fabulous creativity.

● **OPEN:** All year, except January. Weekends only off
season.
● **ROOMS:** Seven rooms, all en suite
● **PRICE:** B&B €85-€100 per person sharing, €40
single supplement
● **NOTES:**
Visa, Mastercard, Laser. Dinner in restaurant Thu-
Sat. Dinner Sun in summer & bank hols. One sitting,
8-course tasting menu, €65. ♿ No disabled access.
Private car parking. Not suitable for children.
● **DIRECTIONS:**
On the R668 Cahir to Lismore road.

# CLIFF HOUSE HOTEL

**Adriaan Bartels**
**Ardmore**
**County Waterford**
☎ **+353 24 87 800**
✉ **info@thecliffhousehotel.com**
🖰 **www.thecliffhousehotel.com**

## Backed up by a great team, Martin Kajuiter is making the magic in Cliff House Hotel.

Writing about contemporary Dutch cooking has become a mainstay of the weekend 'papers and the travel magazines over the last while, but Martin Kajuiter was cooking up a storm in Ardmore long before the latest crew of Dutch cooks made it into print. In many ways, however, it's unfair to say that Kajuiter is a contemporary Dutch chef … he is from Holland, but it is his pristine Waterford and regional ingredients that anchor his cooking, and he has a broad palette of influences, not least great French chefs such as Michel Bras, whose colourful, narrative-driven natural cooking is alive and well in Kajuiter's capable hands. In the gorgeous rooms of the Cliff House Hotel, Mr Kajuiter has the perfect gallery in which to present his artful cooking, because the hotel itself is an architectural and design jewel, so food and aesthetics combine in a winning embrace here. Ladies and gentlemen, they even fold the loo paper in an artful way in the Cliff House. When you pay that sort of attention to detail, it's no surprise that success comes quickly, and Adriaan Bartels and his team are enjoying deserved success and acclaim.

- **OPEN:** all year except Christmas
- **ROOMS:** 39 rooms
- **PRICE:** B&B from €200 per room

- **NOTES:** All major cards accepted. ♿ Disabled access. Restaurant open for dinner, Tue-Sat, €68-€95. Bar serves food noon-9pm. Loc8 code YSB-80-TR9

- **DIRECTIONS:**
From the N25 turn onto the R673 signposted Ardmore. Once in Ardmore take the Middle Road to the hotel. GPS 51.948614 -7.715078

## GLASHA FARMHOUSE

Olive O'Gorman
Ballymacarbry
County Waterford

📱 **+353 52 613 6108**
✉️ **glasha@eircom.net**
🖱️ **www.glashafarmhouse.com**

# So, read on and see if you too agree with the conclusions of Frank and Kitty when it comes to Glasha.

Okay: here we go. Take it away, Frank and Kitty:
'The most wonderful experience ever.'
'We thought we were in heaven.'
'A fab place to chill out.'
'Greatest breakfast ever.'
'Great hospitality.'
Blimey! Was that a good stay in Olive O'Gorman's famous farmhouse B&B, Glasha, or what? Is it the stunning location, between the Comeragh and Knockmealdown Mountains? Is it the intoxication of clean mountain air as you hillwalk and get back in touch with nature, with your body, with the elements? Is it the fishing, the cycling, the golf? (It's not the golf!)
It's all these things but, above all, it's Mrs O'Gorman and the way she will look after you. That's what is really at the core of Frank and Kitty's ecstatic mail to us here at Guides central. That's why Glasha is always full at weekends, with people who have come back for more O'Gorman magic. People come here to get married, to chill, to eat, to enjoy hospitality. They come to Glasha for a piece of heaven.

● **OPEN:** Jan-Dec
● **ROOMS:** Six rooms, all en suite
● **PRICE:** B&B €50-€60 per person sharing.
Single supplement €60-€70

● **NOTES:** Visa, Mastercard, Laser. Dinner 7pm-8.30pm €35-€45. Children over 12 years welcome. Secure parking. ♿ Disabled access.

● **DIRECTIONS:**
Well signposted, off the R671 between Clonmel and Dungarvan. 3km from Ballymacarbry.
GPS 52.276058 -7.759528

# RICHMOND HOUSE

**Paul & Claire Deevy**
**Cappoquin**
**County Waterford**
☎ +353 58 54278
✉ info@richmondhouse.net
🖱 www.richmondhouse.net

## A calm, courteous, dignity underpins all that Paul and Claire Deevy do.

The McKennas had all driven from West Cork to Cappoquin for the launch of Esther Barron's book on the history of Barron's Bakery, one of the food icons of County Waterford and, when we arrived at Richmond, we sat down in the drawing room and had fresh, warm scones and homemade jam and a pot of tea. The fire blazed away, the comfort was as palpable as the sense of welcome. Was there ever such a happy bunch of travellers, so happy to have arrived at their destination, in such a happy place as Richmond House? Out of such precious, unexpected moments, moments of thoughtfulness and generosity, spring a lifetime's worth of happy recollections, and that is exactly what Paul and Claire Deevy specialise in, in this lovely country house. They are elemental, thoughtful people. They and their team look after you, and make sure you have everything you could possibly need, from the tea and scones on arrival, to Paul's delicious and creative country cooking at dinner in the restaurant, and then their delicious breakfasts to set you up for the day. Richmond is a special place, a place where time takes its time.

● **OPEN:** All year except Christmas
● **ROOMS:** Nine rooms
● **PRICE:** from €50 per person sharing, Single supplement €20

● **NOTES:**
All major cards accepted. Restaurant open for dinner, Mon-Sun and Sun lunch. Early bird menu also available. Private parking. Children welcome, babysitting, toys.

● **DIRECTIONS:**
Just outside Cappoquin, the house is well signposted. GPS 52.139261 -7.846708

# THE TANNERY TOWNHOUSE

**Paul & Máire Flynn**
**10 Quay Street, Dungarvan**
**County Waterford**
📱 **+353 58 45420**
📧 **tannery@cablesurf.com**
🖱 **www.tannery.ie**

*A night in the Townhouse,*
*with dinner in the Restaurant,*
*is one of the great events.*

The Tannery Townhouse is a dreamy place. Last time we stayed, in the rooms up above the cookery school, we spent a whole whack of time just taking photographs – get a shot of the window shutters! have you taken one of the pillows! must get one of the bedside lights! I love that French-style garden table!

In between taking photos, we enjoyed incredible cooking in the restaurant – celeriac soup with crispy beef; brandade of smoked haddock with crispy hen's egg; pan-fried cod with mouclade of mussels, leek and ginger; baked skate with with garlic, parsley and romesco sauce; rhubarb tart with yogurt ice cream and walnut crumble; blood orange alaska with candied almonds. The service was pitch-perfect, the value for money was incredible. Back in our lovely room, we concluded that the extraordinary thing about Paul and Maire Flynn is that they do things in a unique way. No one else has rooms like these. No one else concocts their great bedroom breakfasts. No one else cooks the way they cook. They are true sports of nature. They are one of the glories of Irish hospitality.

● **OPEN:** All year, except late January
● **ROOMS:** 14 rooms, all en suite
● **PRICE:** from €50 per person sharing, Single €70

● **NOTES:** Visa, Mastercard, Laser, Amex. Tannery Restaurant is open for dinner Tue-Sat, 6pm-9.30pm. Lunch Fri & Sun. Cookery School.

● **DIRECTIONS:**
20m from The Tannery Restaurant, beside the Old Market House building.
GPS 52.08864 -7.61677

# LOUGH BISHOP HOUSE

**Helen & Christopher Kelly
Derrynagarra, Colinstown
County Westmeath**
☎ + 353 44 966 1313
✉ chkelly@eircom.net
🖰 www.loughbishophouse.com

There is no other farm like Lough Bishop, an aesthete's dream of an Irish farm.

Lily. Patricia. Gwen. Hilda. Viola. Sweetheart. Go on, have a guess? Who are we talking about? The newest Sugababes? Discarded members of Destiny's Child? The latest Girls Aloud? The girls in Beyoncé's band? No, it's something much more important than that. We are talking about the Irish Moiled cows and heifers that you might meet at Helen and Christopher's idyllic Lough Bishop House. Along with Irish Draught horses, Helen and Chris breed Irish Moiled cattle and, along with Jersey and Kerry cows, they are surely the most beautiful things munching in a field near to you. That's the thing about Helen and Christopher: everything they do has an aesthetic edge, so the cows aren't just gorgeous, they even have sweet, Edwardian-style names – a cow named Hilda! This is typical of Lough Bishop, a gorgeous place and, for us, the ultimate Irish agri-turismo. Lough Bishop is a true demonstration farm, for it demonstrates how farming can be a cultural and aesthetic practice, it shows how a farm can be an idyll, a place where time moves at agricultural time. There's nowhere like Lough Bishop.

● **OPEN:** All year, except Christmas and New Year
● **ROOMS:** Three rooms, including family room
● **PRICE:** B&B €55 per person sharing, €25 single supplement

● **NOTES:** No credit cards. Dinner, 7pm, (book before noon), €30. Working farm. ♿ No disabled access.

● **DIRECTIONS:**
From Castlepollard take the R394 Mullingar road, turn left opposite Whitehall School and Church, L5738. 2km up that road on the right-hand side.
GPS 53.6344166 -7.26471666

# WINEPORT LODGE

**Jane English & Ray Byrne**
**Glassan, Athlone**
**County Westmeath**
📱 **+353 90 643 9010**
📧 **lodge@wineport.ie**
🖱 **www.wineport.ie**

## Ray Byrne is one of the great hoteliers, and his ambition and skill fires up his team to do their darndest.

Babymoon. No, we hadn't heard of it either, until we saw that Babymoon breaks are one of the special getaways that Ray and Jane offer in The Wineport. A Babymoon is a final chance for a couple to get away together before junior arrives, and the pitter-patter of tiny feet reshapes your life in ways you had never imagined. Go for it! We're not sure if there is such a thing as a Teenagemoon, but we would sure be game ball for one and, now that we have mentioned it, we are sure that Ray Byrne will invent just such a package for the exhausted parents of teenagers. Mr Byrne is not just one of the great hoteliers of his generation, for he is also one of the most creative, inventive and disciplined hoteliers of his generation. We have followed his career in our books since long before Wineport was ever created, and he has always been the most perspicacious, forward-looking operator. In Wineport, he marshals a superb team, and so everything here is as good as it can be, as good as they can make it, not least the superb modern Irish cooking of chef Cathal Moran, which is amongst the best cooking to be found in the Midlands.

● **OPEN:** All year
● **ROOMS:** 29 rooms
● **PRICE:** B&B from €79 per person sharing. Upgrades and weekend breaks also available.

● **NOTES:** All major cards accepted. Restaurant serves dinner, à la carte 4-course menu, approx €50. ♿ Disabled access.

● **DIRECTIONS:**
At Athlone, take the Longford exit off Dublin/Galway road, fork left at the Dog & Duck. Lodge is 1.5km further on, on the left. GPS 53.465578 -7.883470

117

# KELLY'S RESORT HOTEL

**Bill Kelly**
**Rosslare**
**County Wexford**
📞 **+353 53 913 2114**
✉ **info@kellys.ie**
🖱 **www.kellys.ie**

*Eugene O'Callaghan is one of the great chefs, and Kelly's is one of the great hotels.*

In the middle of his culinary journey towards Beaches Restaurant in Kelly's Resort Hotel, Eugene Callaghan took one of the most unlikely detours in Irish restaurant history. Do you remember it? For a time in the mid 1990's, he cooked from a Portakabin, beside a pub and a chipper, in Ballyedmond, in County Wexford. His unpropitious circumstances didn't make a jot of difference to his cooking: his food was serene, and so was he, and he was the hottest ticket in Wexford for a year or more, until he moved on. He cooked from a Portakabin, and he made it The Savoy. Mr Callaghan's cooking has always had the gift of being able to make every dish he cooks seem definitive, authoritative, complete. He knows food, he knows cooking, and he knows it in a way that is different to any other Irish chef. His food is about food, in the way Maurice Ravel's music, for example, is about music: it is knowing, but so supremely controlled that you don't see the back-story. Beaches is just the right setting for his work – elegant; serene; artistic; comfortable and cosseting, and superbly managed by the Kelly family. One of the greats.

- ● **OPEN:** Feb-early Dec
- ● **ROOMS:** 118 rooms, all en suite
- ● **PRICE:** Spring/autumn: weekend €295pp; 5-day midweek from €550pp; Summer: 7-day rate from €975pp. Shorter breaks available. All full board.

- ● **NOTES:** All major cards accepted. La Marine restaurant also recommended. ♿ Disabled access. Every facility for children & babies.

- ● **DIRECTIONS:**
Clearly signposted in Rosslare.

## McMENAMIN'S

**Seamus & Kay McMenamin**
**6 Glena Terrace**
**Spawell Road, Wexford**
📱 **+ 353 (0) 53-914 6442**
📧 **info@wexford-bedandbreakfast.com**
🖱 **www.wexford-bedandbreakfast.com**

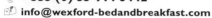

## McMenamin's is as polished and professional a B&B as you will find anywhere in the world.

Some people know just how to push the right buttons. Seamus and Kay McMenamin are two of those people. When they opened their B&B they brought to it a lifetime's worth of experience in the hospitality business, and it shows. Other hosts are generous amateurs, but the McMenamins are generous professionals. They can read your mind. They know that you really crave baked lamb's kidneys cooked in sherry for your breakfast, but would be too shy to ask for them. So, they chalk it up on the blackboard, and then Seamus will persuade you that baked lamb's kidneys in sherry is what you really feel like this morning. And you will agree, and that extra special breakfast will linger in your memory for years as a symbol of the perfect indulgence in the perfect moment on a perfect morning at McMenamin's.

Creating that special moment is what Seamus and Kay do, and their cosy, classic house is the perfect backdrop for one of the best B&B experiences you can enjoy in Ireland. They push the right buttons every time and, like true professionals, you are hardly aware that they are doing it.

● **OPEN:** Mar-Dec
● **ROOMS:** Four rooms
● **PRICE:** B&B from €45-€50 per person sharing

● **NOTES:**
Visa, Mastercard, Laser.
No dinner.
♿ Disabled access.

● **DIRECTIONS:**
In the centre of Wexford, opposite the County Hall.

## MONART

**Liam Griffin**
**The Still, Enniscorthy**
**County Wexford**
📞 **+353 53 923 8999**
✉ **reservations@monart.ie**
🖱 **www.monart.ie**

Few addresses capture the
zeitgeist of a spa-escape as
well as Monart.

Monart got it right when it opened its handsome doors,
its handsome gates, and it continues to get its alliance of
relaxation and invigoration just right, and all the while
improving with age. 'Monart confounds your expectations,
and therein lies its success', says Eamon Barrett. 'It's a
glitzy, glamorous place, a modern extension added onto
a lovely old building, with electric gates to enter - all of
these things make you expect the worst of Celtic Tiger
"We have built it and therefore it will be brilliant" excess.
In fact, nothing could be further from the truth. At its
core are wonderful staff, who love hospitality to their
fingertips - if you've been before they know what room
you were in, they welcome you back, and they mean it.
The architecture is wonderful, curved wings spanning out
into the woods from the main building and as the grounds
have matured the calmness that is inherent at Monart
has just increased. Everything is kept spick and span and
even if you are not the type of person who likes to spend
a weekend in a robe you will still find much to enjoy at
Monart.' Confounding expectations – that's Monart.

● **OPEN:** All year, except Christmas
● **ROOMS:** 70 rooms
● **PRICE:** €95-€250 per person sharing, from €695
for suite, depending on dates and availability, single
supplement €40

● **NOTES:** Visa, Master, Amex. Dinner, €39.50.
♿ Disabled access. Over 18 yrs only. Spa open 9am-
9pm. No functions. D+ B&B rates quoted, see website.

● **DIRECTIONS:**
Just off the N11 road to Gorey. See map on their website. GPS 52.513889 -6.613889

# BALLYKNOCKEN HOUSE

**Catherine Fulvio**
**Glenealy, Ashford**
**County Wicklow**
📱 **+353 404 44627**
📩 **info@ballyknocken.com**
🖱 **www.ballyknocken.com**

## Catherine Fulvio's energy and creativity is the backbone of the beautiful Ballyknocken House.

'I'm a real Wicklow woman', Catherine Fulvio told the travel writer Pól O Conghaile. Indeed she is. The married name may be Italian, but Mrs Fulvio's maiden name is Catherine Byrne and what she does in Ballyknocken is simply continuing the family business, running a B&B and restaurant – and a cookery school – which dates back to 1969, when her mum first took in guests.

We have known Mrs Fulvio since long before she took over at Ballyknocken, and aside from her work ethic, her skills and her efficiency, she has always impressed us as a person who knows, first and foremost, who she is: she is a real Wicklow woman. There is a no-nonsense wisdom to her, a maturity she bestows on Ballyknocken. Her cooking shows this: it's gutsy food that she likes to cook and eat, perfect for folk who have had a busy day doing good work, and there is both purity and simplicity in it, along with the generosity that is an integral, defining part of her work. Breakfasts are as delicious as dinner, with all the meals bringing the true tastes of Wicklow to the table. Ballyknocken is a great destination, the real thing.

- ● **OPEN:** mid Feb-mid Dec
- ● **ROOMS:** Seven rooms
- ● **PRICE:** From €55-€59 per person sharing.

- ● **NOTES:** Visa, Mastercard. Dinner, Fri, Sat €45.
  ♿ No disabled access.
  Cookery school.

- ● **DIRECTIONS:**
From Dublin, head south to Ashford (on N11), then turn right after Chester Beatty pub. Continue for 5km and the house is on the right.
GPS N52°58.6674 W006°8.6322

# THE BROOK LODGE INN

**Evan Doyle**
**Macreddin Village, Aughrim**
**County Wicklow**
☎ **+353 402 36444**
✉ **brooklodge@macreddin.ie**
🖰 **www.brooklodge.com**

No challenge is too great, no demand too steep, for the team at the Brook Lodge Inn.

Well, we said to ourselves, just how is Evan Doyle going to pull this one off? One course of the extensive Wild & Slow menu to celebrate the Brook Lodge's annual festival featured "Wild Sea Beet Laverbreads". But laverbreads aren't made with sea beet, so Mr Doyle was setting himself a challenge of getting something good to go with smoked wild River Nore salmon and some lovely pickled wild marsh samphire. Of course, he pulled it off with gas in the tank: the beets were cooked then coated in organic oats from Kilbeggan and crisped. They were superb, and they were superb with the fish and the samphire. But then pulling rabbits out of top-hats is what Mr Doyle and his team do, day after day, event after event. The Wild & Slow dinner featured a menu composed entirely of wild ingredients cooked for 200 people! 200! Anyone else would tell you that was an impossible thing to achieve. But, to mangle that old advertising slogan, impossible is nothing to this team. Impossible is where they start, and their ambition makes The Brook Lodge and The Strawberry Tree truly special places, special and unique.

- **OPEN:** All year, excluding Christmas
- **ROOMS:** 86 bedrooms and suites
- **PRICE:** B&B from €55 per person sharing, single supplement €30. Also web offers.
- **NOTES:** All major cards accepted. Two restaurants, pub, market and bakery. Secure car parking. Reservations essential. ♿ Limited disabled access.
- **DIRECTIONS:**
From Rathdrum, take the R753 to Aughrim. When you arrive in Aughrim, turn right at church and follow signs. Note: do not follow a sat nav, as it will send you over the mountains.

**10 PLACES**

# WITH HOT RESTAURANTS

**1**

### THE BROOK LODGE INN
### COUNTY WICKLOW

**2**

### BROOK'S HOTEL
### COUNTY DUBLIN

**3**

### GREGAN'S CASTLE
### COUNTY CLARE

**4**

### MOUNT JULIET
### COUNTY KILKENNY

**5**

### SPRINGFORT HALL
### COUNTY CORK

**6**

### STEP HOUSE HOTEL
### COUNTY CARLOW

**7**

### THE TWELVE HOTEL
### COUNTY GALWAY

**8**

### THE TANNERY
### COUNTY WATERFORD

**9**

### VIEWMOUNT HOUSE
### COUNTY LONGFORD

**10**

### WILD HONEY INN
### COUNTY CLARE

# BEECH HILL HOUSE HOTEL

**Patsey O'Kane**
**Londonderry**
**County Londonderry**
📞 **+44 28 7134 9279**
📧 **info@beech-hill.com**
🖰 **www.beech-hill.com**

## The Beech Hill is one of the great Irish hotels, and Patsey O'Kane and her team bring an instinctive hospitality.

We are great admirers of Patsey O'Kane, an hotelier who is one of the great figures of Northern Irish hospitality. Ms O'Kane incarnates that true hospitality which the people of Northern Ireland exude, and she frames it within the rigour of acute professionalism, and within the lovely aesthetic of the Beech Hill House itself.

Ms O'Kane is to Northern hospitality what Myrtle Allen is to Southern hospitality: an original, a person of true conviction, a shining, modest star who never goes off message, and whose message is true and consistent. What makes the Beech Hill special is simple, and utterly fundamental: everyone in the hotel over-delivers, everyone is always trying to do their best, to make sure that every detail is done right, done as well as it can be. That is the art of hotel keeping, that is the very essence of the art we look for in the McKennas' Guides, and Ms O'Kane is mistress of that art and practices that art every day in her work in this beautiful, early 18th-century house. Beech Hill is two miles from Derry but, actually, it is a place unto itself, a palace of hospitality. Give this woman a peerage.

- **OPEN:** All year, except 24-25 Dec
- **ROOMS:** 30 rooms and suites
- **PRICE:** B&B £62.50-£117.50 per person sharing, £95-£105 single B&B

- **NOTES:**
All major cards accepted. Ardmore Restaurant open for lunch and dinner. ♿ Disabled access
- **DIRECTIONS:**
On the A6 direction in Londonderry, take the turning at Faughan Bridge. Travel 1 mile to Ardmore Chapel, where you will see the hotel entrance on your left.

# THE CARRIAGE HOUSE

**Maureen Griffith**
**71 Main Street, Dundrum**
**County Down**
📱 **+44 28 4375 1635**
📠 **inbox@carriagehousedundrum.com**
🖱 **www.carriagehousedundrum.com**

*north*
*east*
*west*
*south*

Maureen Griffith has the
true artist's eye, and her
vision permeates everything.

Paul Klee is in The Carriage House. Not exactly physi-
cally, not corporally, if you know what we mean. What
we mean is that one of the rooms in Maureen Griffith's
gorgeous house is named for the great artist: 'Klee' it says
on the little pottery tile on the door, and there is also
'Homer' – we'd wager it's some dude other than Mr Simp-
son – and 'Croft', named after the painter Richard Croft.
We have described Mrs Griffith's house as enjoying a
'visual palette', but the aesthetic is not simply 'painterly'
as  we have said: it's actually deeper than that. There is an
appreciation of aesthetics in every aspect of everything in
the house, from the names of the rooms to the apposite-
ness of the open-plan sitting and dining rooms downstairs. Such a deep understanding of colour, of fabrics, of
texture, of quirkiness, makes for a house that is a comfort
classic, at the same time as being a design classic. Getting
those two things so right is an amazing achievement, but
then Mrs Griffith is an amazing woman. So, sit us down in
the drawing room, feed us some fabulous tea and cakes,
and let us revel in the sheer beauty of this great house.

● **OPEN:** All year
● **ROOMS:** Three rooms, all en suite
● **PRICE:** B&B £65 Double, £70 Twin, £45 Single

● **NOTES:** No credit cards. No dinner, but two
excellent restaurants, adjacent to building. Storage for
guests' bicycles. ♿No disabled access, bedrooms on
second floor.

● **DIRECTIONS:**
Dundrum is on the main Belfast to Newcastle road
(A24), and The Carriage House is in the centre of
town. Postcode BT33 0LU

# DUFFERIN COACHING INN

**Leontine Haines**
**Killyleagh**
**County Down**
📱 **+44 28 4482 1134**
📧 **info@dufferincoachinginn.com**
🖲 **www.dufferincoachinginn.com**

## Leontine Hayes has solved the problem of what to do with all our old bank buildings: open them as inns!

Leontine Haines got all the details right before opening her doors in this lovely, early 19th-century coaching house in pretty Killyleagh. Part of the building was formerly a bank but, unlike most Irish banks, Ms Haines actually knows how to run a business properly and professionally. The rooms and bathrooms are beautifully appointed, the towels are fluffy, the Bircher muesli at breakfast is as scrumptious as all the other home-made ingredients that comprise the feast that starts the day.

Many guests who stay at the Dufferin choose to eat next door to the Inn, at the friendly Dufferin Arms, where the cooking is good. A wise choice, however, is to head to nearby Balloo House, where the brilliant Danny Millar cooks up a culinary storm, with some of the most inventive cooking in Ireland. Leontine seems to us to get better each year as word spreads about this special house, a destination that is another feather in the cap of this lovely village in this lovely region. Wine buffs, by the way, shouldn't miss a visit to Jim Nicholson's wine shop in nearby Crossgar, the most beautiful wine shop in Ireland.

● **OPEN:** All year
● **ROOMS:** Seven rooms, all en suite
● **PRICE:** B&B £65-£90 per room (£45-£65 for single occupancy)

● **NOTES:**
All major cards accepted.
♿ No disabled access.

● **DIRECTIONS:**
Killyleagh is 16 miles, half an hour's drive, from Belfast, and the Inn is in the town centre, next to the Dufferin Arms.

128

# MARLAGH LODGE

**Robert & Rachel Thompson**
**71 Moorfields Road, Ballymena**
**County Antrim**
📱 **+44 28 2563 1505**
📧 **info@marlaghlodge.com**
🖰 **www.marlaghlodge.com**

*Rachel Thompson is one
of the best modern cooks
working in the North.*

When we were writing the text for the places to stay and
eat for *The Irish Times* Great Drives app – you can get it at
www.irishtimes.com/mobile – one of the drives created
by Bob Montgomery was on the A43, around the Glen of
Antrim.

Well, that was an easy one to do, we said to ourselves:
if you are up exploring the Glens, if you are motoring
your way around the North Antrim coast, then you will
be staying and eating at Marlagh Lodge. It is as simple as
that. Starting from a near-ruin, and less than a decade ago,
Robert and Rachel Thompson have resurrected, renovated and restored a stunningly beautiful house, with appo-
site period details in every room. What is equally stunning
is Rachel's glorious cooking, with every dish both graceful
and flavour-filled, carefully sourced and cooked, enjoyed
in the William Morris-style room by candlelight, with a
bottle of wine from James Nicholson's wine merchants
to add to the pleasure. Could anything be nicer after a
day driving through the Glens? No sir. Mrs Thompson is a
true cook, with verve and style in every dish she prepares.

● **OPEN:** Open all year, except Christmas
● **ROOMS:** Three rooms, all en suite
● **PRICE:** B&B £45 per person. No single supplement

● **NOTES:**
Mastercard, Visa, Switch, Maestro. Dinner, 8pm £35
(book by noon). ♿ No disabled access.

● **DIRECTIONS:**
From the A36 to Larne, turn onto Rankinstown Road,
and the driveway is immediately on your left.
GPS 54.846111 -6.226944

132

**CONTACT THE McKENNAS:**

We greatly appreciate receiving reports, e-mails and criticisms from readers, and would like to thank those who have written in the past, whose opinions are of enormous assistance to us when considering which 100 places finally make it into this book.

Our website has two contact forms - one to contact us, and the other to make recommendations.

We love hearing from you.

**www.guides.ie**